MW00898560

Healing the Wounds of Anger in Marriage

Real Skills for Positive Relationship Change

Book and Workbook for Couples

© Copyright 2015 by Lynette J. Hoy, NCC, LCPC, CAMS-IV
&
Ted Griffin, Editor/writer
Steve Yeschek, Contributor

A CounselCare Connection Publication
Oak Brook, Illinois
www.counselcareconnection.org

May be purchased at the
Anger Management Institute shopping mall:
www.whatsgoodaboutanger.com

Healing the Wounds of Anger in Marriage

Real Skills for Positive Relationship Change

Book and Workbook for Couples

Copyright © 2015 by Lynette J. Hoy and Ted Griffin;
Contributor: Steve Yeschek
Adapted from What's Good About Anger? first, second, third edition books.

Requests for information should be addressed to:
CounselCare Connection, P.C.
1200 Harger Rd., Suite 602
Oak Brook, Illinois, 60523

ISBN   978-1517177935

CounselCare Connection Publications
Oak Brook, Illinois
Printed in the United States of America

To my lovely wife Lois, for her gracious patience and persevering love, without which I might never have chosen to allow God to bring my anger under his control.
    Ted Griffin

To my husband, David, who has inspired and encouraged me and demonstrated God's love to me for over 46 years.
    Lynette J. Hoy

TABLE OF CONTENTS

Hoy/Griffin ©2015   www.whatsgoodaboutanger.com

Healing the Wounds of Anger in Marriage –
Couples Anger Management Book and Workbook

Dear Spouse/Partner,
Welcome to the What's Good About Anger? course for couples! As you complete the readings and workbook lessons -- we hope that you will discover new information about anger, how to manage it and how to express anger in healthy ways -- ways which will build up your relationship and marriage. Most likely, you have experienced harmful anger within your marriage. This may have resulted in feelings of hurt, disappointment, resentment and mistrust. This course is geared to focus on how your approach to anger affects your marriage or relationship and then, how to make the healthy and helpful changes which will also bring about healing for any previous wounds and resentments.

Start out by completing the survey in lesson one, log any scenarios and your typical response to anger. This will help you discover what makes you angry, which coping skills and new approaches to apply to your life and relationship to manage it effectively. Each lesson contains some particular questions or activities for you to work through personally and questions to discuss as a couple.

Reflect on this question: *What makes people angry?* Numerous answers may come to mind such as:

> Differences of opinion,
> Personality clashes,
> Expectations,
> Blocked goals,
> Low self-esteem,
> Depression, grief, mental health disorders,
> Loss of hope and control,
> Health problems,
> Conflict,
> Job dissatisfaction,
> Financial pressures,
> Stress,
> Family or relationship issues.

Anger is a common emotion for everyone and thus, you will find through your reading that many people experience anger in various ways and for various reasons: people who are depressed or withdrawn; those who tend to hold in their feelings, hurt and anger; people who lash out and are aggressive when they feel angry or those who lack skills or self-control. Often it is taught that anger is not an acceptable emotion or experience – especially for religious people. Through this course we hope you will come to understand and experience: *Healing from the wounds of anger in your marriage and how to apply real skills for positive relational change!*

Hoy/Griffin ©2015 www.whatsgoodaboutanger.com

Overview:

This new book/workbook compilation provides a fresh look at anger and explores how this emotion -- usually viewed as negative -- can be transformed into faith, assertiveness, problem-solving, conflict resolution, empathy, and forgiveness. Each lesson includes activities and couple's questions. This edition adds thoughtful questions geared to bring resolution and healing to the hurts and resentments that often occur in relationships.

Chronic anger can be costly -- physically, emotionally and relationally. Most people can use their anger in appropriate ways in some situations, and yet can be ineffectual or harmful in other situations. You and your partner may have suffered destructive consequences due to anger and conflict in your relationship such as: defensiveness, stone-walling, hurtful words, abusiveness or emotional distance.

Participation in this course often reduces levels of anger and helps partners learn to turn anger into productive behaviors and positive attitudes. You can learn effective coping behaviors to stop escalation, resolve conflicts and restore intimacy. Logging anger, triggering situations and applying new coping approaches will help you to more effectively control the unhealthy anger responses which are causing problems, conflict and resentment in your marriage or relationship.

- Identifying triggers,
- Logging scenarios,
- Applying new skills such as: time-outs, prayer,
- Addressing issues with assertiveness,
- Establishing a plan of action,
- Making requests,
- Learning to problem-solve,
- Getting guidance from a pastor or counselor when needed,
- Changing self-talk,
- Conflict resolution,
- Stress management,
- Relaxation techniques,
- Emotional Intelligence & Empathy skills,
- Turning anger into forgiveness,
- Managing stress and conflict,
- Applying HEALING Steps,
- Dealing with control issues,
- Taking responsibility,
- Stopping blame.

The What's Good About Anger? anger management course employs these major areas and anger control interventions.

Here are the instructions for as you use the What's Good About Anger? Course and couple's workbook

1. Complete the Anger Survey. This will help you assess when, where and *how* you get angry and your general provocation scenario (GPS). Be honest about your feelings and experience with anger. After all, this course-work is personal and geared to help you get an understanding of how you can grow in tackling any problem you may be having with anger in your life and in your relationships.

2. Complete the Anger Management Progress Report each week to keep track of any improvements you are making. Especially note how your relationship is affected or changed.

3. View the DVD if you have purchased it and read through the corresponding lessons. Complete the questions as you progress. Apply your general provocation scenario (found in the Anger Survey) to the section in the course on Handling Anger Effectively.

4. Keep an anger log throughout the time you are reading this book. Each day think about and try one or two of the suggestions for handling anger. Especially apply the steps in Handling Anger Effectively to each situation. Write out your basic concerns, your options and requests.

5. Carefully, read through the chapters on stress management, assertiveness and conflict resolution. Apply these skills to your personal life and relationship. Be specific about the situations you regularly encounter with your partner and apply the recommended skills to those situations which will enhance healthy conflict resolution.

6. The chapter on When to Take a Time-Out will help you make a plan for the situations that come up that cause your anger to escalate more quickly and you to feel out of control. If you still find your anger escalating, then lengthen your time-out period (Example: one hour instead of 30 minutes). Note the Time-Out procedure and couple agreement found in this workbook.

7. Evaluate your thinking with the cognitive distortions questions and log your thinking patterns. This exercise will help you identify any false perspective you have about your partner or situations and challenge whether it is correct.

8. Take the empathy inventory - completing the lesson: How Emotional Intelligence Impacts Anger.

9. Complete the Plan to Change Your Life By Changing Your Thinking and summary.

10. Read and complete the lessons on Steps for HEALING the Wounds of Anger in Your Marriage. Take time to role-play and practice each step. Additional aspects of this course will encourage you to apply skills and concepts related to: forgiveness, assertiveness, problem-solving, empathy, taking responsibility, defusing anger, building relationships and foundational principles. These strategies will help you to effectively manage anger – preventing damage from harmful anger.

11. **Your relationship**: Throughout this workbook some questions and activities are geared for discussion or to work through as a couple. Activities and questions are included. These are geared to bring resolution and healing to hurts and resentments in relationships

We encourage you to be positive to refrain from making negative comments about your partner and to take responsibility for your own actions. *You are the only person you can change.* Your partner is the only one who can change herself/himself. You will find this workbook most helpful if you approach it with openness to learning and a willingness to apply some of the skills to your life.

*Warning: if you are in an abusive relationship – we encourage you to call the domestic violence hotline for guidance: 1-800-799-7233 and visit: www.saferelationships.net *There is no excuse for abuse in any relationship.*

All aspects of this course will encourage you to apply helpful strategies and foundational principles to your life so you can not only achieve healing in your marriage but, *put your anger to work for good – building a more satisfying relationship!*

Now – let's get started by completing the anger survey on the next page.

ANGER SURVEY copyright © 2012 by Lynette J. Hoy, NCC, LCPC and Ted Griffin, Editor/writer
Please answer the following questions as accurately and as completely as possible.

Rate the severity of your anger:
Question 1:

1. **How often do you get angry?** (Circle one that applies)
(a) daily.
(b) many times a day.
(c) a few times a month.
(d) several times a week.
(e) very rarely.

(a) 4
(b) 5
(c) 2
(d) 3
(e) 1

2. **What happens when you get angry?** (Circle all that apply)
I tend to:
(a) feel tense.
(b) withdraw.
(c) exercise.
(d) feel sick.
(e) overeat.
(f) distract myself.
(g) tell someone.
(h) raise my voice.
(i) hit someone or something.
(j) become cynical or sarcastic.
(k) take a time-out.
(l) think about how to get even.
(m) avoid the issue.
(n) make light of things or joke.
(o) pray.
(p) other_____.
(q) go out drinking.
(r) argue.
(s) talk it over.
(t) swear.
(u) feel depressed.

Question 2:

(a) 1
(b) 3
(c) 1
(d) 3
(e) 3
(f) 1
(g) 1
(h) 4
(i) 5
(j) 4
(k) 1
(l) 4
(m) 3
(n) 3
(o) 0
(p) 3 (if a negative or harmful response)
(q) 5
(r) 4
(s) 1
(t) 4
(u) 4

Total your scores from questions 1 and 2 together.
Assess the Category You Are In:
Category I: 1-10 points =little problem with anger.
Category II: 10-20 points =moderate problem.
*If either Category I or II includes trouble with the law, injury to others or self, drinking, depression, outbursts, experiencing anger several times a day, etc. then, you have a serious -- Category III -- problem with anger.
Category III: 20 points and above =serious problem with anger.
Resource: What's Good About Anger? copyright © 2012 by Lynette J. Hoy, NCC, LCPC and Ted Griffin, Editor/writer

3. **Which people tend to trigger your anger?** (check all that apply):

___(a) significant others.

___(b) co-workers.

___(c) policemen.

___(d) boss.

___(e) friends.

___(f) strangers.

___(g) men.

___(h) women.

___(i) others: _____.

4.**What situations or behavior tend to trigger your anger?** (check all that apply):

When people:

___(a) treat me unfairly.

___(b) disrespect me.

___(c) ignore me.

___(d) put me down.

___(e) threaten me.

___(f) interrupt me.

___(g) keep me waiting.

___(h) joke about me.

___(i) hit me.

When I am:

___(j) working.

___(k) disappointed with someone.

___(l) missing someone.

___(m) experiencing loss or change.

___(n) under stress.

___(o) late to events.

___(p) unable to achieve my goals.

___(q) unable to share my opinions.

___(r) bored.

___(s) in a crisis.

___(t) Other: _____.

Write out a recent situation when you felt angry:
What happened?

Where was it? How long did you feel angry?

With whom were you angry?

How did you react?

5. Where are you most likely to get angry? (check all that apply):

___(a) at home.
___(b) at work.
___(c) in social situations.
___(d) during sports or recreation activities.
___(e) driving.
___(f) in public.
___(g) other:_____

6. What happens after you get angry? (check all that apply):

___(a) someone gets hurt.
___(b) I feel guilty.
___(c) my relationships are disrupted.
___(d) I feel defensive.
___(e) I get in trouble with the law.
___(f) I try to make restitution or reconcile with the person.
___(g) I ask God for wisdom and guidance.
___(h) I don't talk to the other person.
___(i) I can't stop thinking about the event/person.
___(j) I get depressed or think about harming myself.
___(k) I lose sleep or can't eat.
___(l) I feel relieved.
___(m) I have been asked to leave.
___(n) I get in trouble at work.
___(o) others say I have a problem with anger.
___(p) I want to run away.
___(q) other: _____.

Rate your answers from question 6 above.

.....You handle anger *pretty well* if you checked only b, f, g and l. Anger is not disrupting your life but, you could be dealing with hidden anger.

.....You are unable to control your anger and your anger is *causing serious interference in* your life and relationships if you checked any of these:

a, c, e, h, i, j, k, m, n, o, p, and (q: if *other* is an unhealthy response).

7. How do you normally help yourself calm down when you feel angry? (check all that apply):

___(a) deep breathing and relaxation techniques.
___(b) prayer.
___(c) counting to ten.
___(d) reading the Bible.
___(e) telling myself: "This is not worth getting angry over."
___(f) thinking about the negative consequences that could result from getting angry and losing control.
___(g) thinking about what the real issue is.

I tell myself:

___(h) "This person is not making sense now. He/she may have had a bad day."
___(i) "I'm going to try to work through this problem reasonably."
___(j) "I should try to cooperate -- he 's/she's making sense."
___(k) "Maybe I should take a time-out until I cool down."
___(l) "I should try to understand what this person is upset about by listening and paraphrasing."
Other things you say or do to control yourself or the situation:_____

General Provocation Scenario: In the space below write out a typical situation which you find yourself getting annoyed or angry which includes your partner. Pretend it is a play. Describe what happened, who was involved, when and where it happened and what transpired beforehand. Then write out what each person said and did and what you thought, communicated and how you acted.

Who:

Where:

When:

What led up to this scene:

The scene opens:

What I think:

What I do:

What I say:

What other person says/docs:

How did you recently control or not control your anger?

Write out: What happened?

What triggered your angry response?

What were the circumstances?

What were your thoughts?

What were you telling yourself?

Who else was involved?

Log Your Anger:

Write down the situations when you get angry, and rate them:

1. When did you last feel angry?

2. What happened and with whom?

3. What were you thinking when this occurred?
Example: "He/she never understands." "I am just a failure." "I can't handle this." "He/she doesn't care about me." "This situation is hopeless." "I will never succeed." "My partner meant to ignore me." "This project is dead in the water." "I couldn't have done a worse job." "That person never should have cut me off." "If I had just prayed more, I never would have lost my job." "He/she's such a loser."

4. Rate the strength of the anger: 1 = lowest; 5 = moderate; 10 = strongest.

        1   2   3   4   5   6   7   8   9   10

5. Continue to keep an anger log for one to two weeks, then, evaluate your angry responses as suggested below.

What could you have changed?

Did you take any time-outs to cool down?

Evaluate your angry response:
How did it affect you? How did it affect your partner?
Was it destructive; did it lead to resentment and a broken relationship?

Did it lead to problem-solving, restoring your relationship, and honest (loving) dialogue?

Did you seek spiritual help or counsel?

What would help you control your anger in the future?

What was your thinking prior to and during the episode of anger? Do you have any of the Cognitive Distortions found in the course?

Now go to "Handling Anger Effectively," and apply your situations to the model given.

Lesson One *Anger's Many Faces*

> **Goal:** To define anger, how it affects people and relationships. To explore triggers for and teaching about anger.

Anger, though potentially harmful, can be transformed into a positive force accomplishing great good in our lives.

Ted Griffin and Lynette Hoy

Lynette's Story

I can remember the day one of my sisters came home with a suspension slip for throwing an orange in the lunchroom. My father dragged her upstairs to the attic. There were loud noises, yelling, and crying. She limped down the stairs, bloody and bruised.
I can remember the beatings in the basement with a board, my father's rage, the pain and the fear.
I can remember experiencing a "cold shoulder" for days when I would disappoint someone in my family.
I can remember my husband and I up in the attic of our second story rented flat, two weeks after our daughter was born, screaming at each other and throwing things. I don't remember what caused the anger or why it hurt so much. But I experienced anger's pain, inner wounds, and loneliness.
I learned that anger was something to be feared, that it was cruel, loud, cold, silent, resentful, and threatening.

Ted's Story

I have long feared anger--my father's and my own. My dad, an alcoholic who's drinking kept him from connecting with his family, had a quiet anger. He didn't beat us or yell at us for hours--he just sort of ignored us. My anger--which was really years' worth of bitterness toward Dad-- became violent, abusive and dangerous, especially after my father died and I couldn't express my anger to the one I was really mad at because he wasn't around anymore.

Looking back, I am ashamed of many of the things I said and did at that stage of my life. And I thank God for helping me forgive my father and learn how to be kind to my family--a family I almost lost because of my rage. Not all anger is wrong, but when it's like mine was, only God can keep the individual and his family from going over the cliff. The journey hasn't been easy or quick, but God has sustained me every step of the way, and He continues to do so. Not everyone turns to faith to deal with their anger, but that is what made the difference in my life.

All of us have experienced anger. Some of us have cringed under the rage in our families, struggled with it in our souls, felt it toward our friends and loved ones. Some of us have shocked others with volcanoes of anger.

But anger is not just a personal enemy. The evidence abounds that we live in a mad, mad, mad world. Statistics from American Demographics tell us:

• 23% of Americans admit they openly express their anger.

• 39% say they hold it in or hide it.

• 23% say they walk away from the situation.

• 23% confess to having hit someone in anger.

• 17% admit they have destroyed the property of someone who made them mad.

We want to demonstrate to you that anger, though potentially harmful, is a complex emotion we can come to understand and a positive force that can accomplish great good in our lives.

What Is Anger?
When you think about anger, what words or pictures come to mind? Frustration? Rage? Anger can be defined as an aversive state ranging from annoyance to rage. Webster's says, "Anger is a strong feeling of displeasure and antagonism, indignation or an automatic reaction to any real or imagined insult, frustration, or injustice, producing emotional agitation seeking expression."

"Most authors agree that anger ranges along a dimension of intensity, from frustration and annoyance to rage. Dutton and colleagues distinguished between "subanger" (frustration, annoyance, and irritation) and anger. As reported by Scheiman, sociological studies have compared the demographic prevalence of three levels of anger: feeling annoyed, feeling angry, and shouting. Anger clearly varies in intensity within an episode. At extreme intensity, people become swept up in their anger, do things they might not otherwise do, and experience these acts as at least partially involuntary... Anger is generally held to be a negative (aversive) emotion, but one that involves active approach, in contrast to the negative emotions of sadness and fear which involve inhibition and withdrawal, respectively. While anger itself is generally negative, it can be accompanied by positive feelings, such as increased alertness, strength, confidence, determination, and pride." International Handbook of Anger by M. Potegal, G. Stemmler, C. Spielberger

Let's look at the problem of anger in our society. Anger's effects are evident. There is rampant violence in schools, families, and neighborhoods. For example:
• Severe violence is a chronic feature of 13% of all marriages and generally 35 violent incidents occur before any type of report is made.
• Every twenty-five seconds someone is a victim of a violent crime such as murder, robbery, assault, or rape.

Anger is one of the most troubling emotions! We sometimes hear blatant admonishments such as "we shouldn't ever be angry." So what happens to our anger? We end up feeling guilty for being angry, or we pretend we're not angry, or we numb our feelings or turn our anger into depression.

"Frustration and anger are normal responses to many negative situations and problems we face in life. Often we have difficulty taking responsibility for and honestly expressing our anger. Sometimes the guilt we feel as a result of being angry builds--causing inner shame and turmoil. Hostility, aggression, resentment, hatred, rage may or may not be manifested or play a part in an angry episode."
R. Potter-Efron

What is Anger Management? Anger Management is the ability to recognize anger and develop and apply skills and abilities to respond in a healthy and socially appropriate manner. Anger management needs to include the evidence-based treatment strategies found in this book.

Foundational Insights:
Anger is an energy or force which is often harmful. Anger is caused by feelings of helplessness and the need to control situations, people and consequences. Anger — when expressed in a healthy way — can foster personal growth and significance, improving relationships and changing lives.

Questions for Thought

1. Do you agree or disagree with the Foundational Insights? What do these statements teach about the underlying reasons for anger?

_____

_____

_____

_____

2. Do you ever get angry? Write out 3 situations in your relationship which most often make you feel angry?

_____

_____

_____

_____

_____

_____

_____

_____

3. How would your life be different if you were to respond to anger in your relationship in a healthy way?

_____

_____

_____

_____

What would YOU need to change?

_____

_____

4. What are your reasons for taking this course? What do you hope to learn?

_____

_____

5. How would you define anger? What pictures or words come to mind when you think of anger?

_____

_____

_____

_____

6. How have you experienced anger in your family of origin? What effect have those experiences had on the anger in your relationship?

_____

_____

7. How do you generally express anger during angry episodes you experience in your marriage/relationship? Write out the consequences of your anger:

_____

_____

_____

_____

_____

8. When have you expressed your anger or frustration in a healthy way in your marriage/relationship? What was the result?

_____

_____

9. Write out a time when you were able to control your anger in your relationship? What was different?

_____

_____

_____

_____

Questions for discussion with your partner: (discuss these questions refraining from negative comments or blaming):

1. What do these insights teach about anger? How does this change or help your perspective about anger?

_____

_____

_____

_____

2. When have you expressed your anger or frustration in a healthy way in your relationship? What was the result?

_____

_____

_____

3. If you could wake up tomorrow and manage your anger – how would it affect your life and relationship? (talk about yourself not your partner here)

_____

_____

_____

*GLOSSARY

Aggression- Behavior intended to cause psychological or physical harm to someone or to a surrogate target. The behavior may be verbal or physical, direct or indirect.

Anger- A negatively toned emotion, subjectively experienced as an aroused state of antagonism toward someone or something perceived to be the source of an aversive event.

Anger control- The regulation of anger activation and its intensity, duration, and mode of expression. Regulation occurs through cognitive, somatic, and behavioral systems.

Anger reactivity- Responding to aversive, threatening, or other stressful stimuli with anger reactions characterized by automaticity of engagement, high intensity, and short latency.

Escalation of provocation- Incremental increases in the probability of anger and aggression, occurring as reciprocally heightened antagonism in an interpersonal exchange.

Frustration- Either a situational blocking or impeding of behavior toward a goal or the subjective feeling of being thwarted in attempting to reach a goal.

Hostility- An attitudinal disposition of antagonism toward another person or social system. It represents a predisposition to respond with aggression under conditions of perceived threat.

Inhibition- A restraining influence on anger expression. The restraint may be associated with either external or internal factors.

Stress inoculation- A three-phased, cognitive-behavioral approach to therapy, involving cognitive preparation/conceptualization, skill acquisition/rehearsal, and application/ follow-through. Cognitive restructuring, arousal reduction, and behavioral coping skills training are the core treatment components. Therapist-guided, graded exposure to stressors occurs in the application phase, where the client's enhanced anger control skills are engaged.

Violence- Seriously injurious aggressive behavior, typically having some larger societal significance. The injury may be immediate or delayed.

Resource: Raymond W. Novaco. Encyclopedia of Psychotherapy, VOLUME 1, Copyright 2002, Elsevier Science (USA).

Hatred- The end product of the resentment process. Hatred is "frozen" anger that results in an intense and unchanging dislike of another.

Lesson Two *The Power of Anger*

Goals: *Identify the process of anger, how anger can be helpful and how it is harmful. Normalize anger and identify triggers provoking anger.*

Anger is a great force. If you control it -- it can be transmuted into a power which can move the whole world.

William Shenstone

Anger can actually be helpful. Anger is like a warning signal alerting you that something is wrong. It can provide the energy to resist emotional or physical threats. Anger can help you mobilize your resources and set appropriate limits and boundaries. Your anger can give you strength to resist threatening demands or a violation of your values.

Anger helps you overcome the fear of asserting your needs and facing conflict. Anger can be used for beneficial purposes.

And yes, anger can be harmful. As Will Rogers quipped, "People who fly into a rage always make a bad landing." William Blake wrote: *"I was angry with my friend. I told my wrath, my wrath did end. I was angry with my foe; I told it not, my wrath did grow."*

Unexpressed anger is not only harmful to you physically, but it plays havoc on your emotions and your spirituality. When you don't talk about your anger and the issue that upsets you, you are pretending that everything is fine and are hiding your true feelings. You end up living a lie. The Good Book says, "having put away falsehood. let each one of you speak the truth with his neighbor, for we are members one of another." [1]

Harmful anger costs you too much physically. It yields the largest increases in heart rate and blood pressure of all emotional reactions. Anger results in ulcers, cardiovascular diseases, colitis, and a depleted immune system. Not only is it damaging to the body, but anger damages mental health and your relationships.

Signs indicating when anger is a problem:
- When it is too frequent.
- When it is too intense.
- When it lasts too long.
- When it leads to aggression.
- When it disturbs work or relationships.

When Anger Wakes Up
To help you understand why it is hard to shake anger after it wakes up, you need to learn the physiological mechanism involved in anger arousal:
When you perceive a threat or provocation, your internal fight/flight response is alerted. Within three seconds your breathing and heart rate increases.

Then a hormonal surge kicks in that lasts thirty minutes. Your long-term anger response can be abbreviated when the early stage of anger arousal is interrupted.

Who's responsible for your anger? People often blame others for their anger or situations which are stressful. But, the truth is--you make the decision to get angry. No one can control you and your feelings. People may try to make you mad, but you make a choice about whether to get angry, laugh, or forget about it.

Anger Triggers

Factors that can impact anger arousal in individuals include the following: Undesirable bodily states actually can increase anger arousal. Fatigue, sleep deprivation, pain, hangovers all lower the threshold of reactivity to an event that can precipitate anger. Premenstrual syndrome and low blood sugar can actually contribute to aggression.

High intakes of sugar trigger a surge of insulin that not only converts sugar just consumed but also other available sugar. This leads to depressed blood sugar levels, resulting in moodiness and triggering irritability and aggression.

Cognitive triggers: The way you perceive an event determines the extent to which you judge it as threatening provocation. Extremely rigid or biased appraisals of events prime you for over-reaction to what might normally be only a slightly irritating incident.

How you create anger:

Anger cycle #1 begins with an event or some stress that leads to Trigger Thoughts:

These cycles are self-perpetuating. Your self-talk can keep your anger simmering.

Here's an example for *anger cycle #1:*

A friend stands you up for a luncheon date, and you begin to think about how this friend has let you down in the past. This triggers hurt and anger and more thoughts about how this friend's behavior has disappointed you, which results in more anger.

Anger cycle #2: Another way to arouse anger is by Trigger Thoughts that actually create some arousal or stress. This results in feelings of anger, which leads to more Trigger Thoughts, creating a stress reaction that fuels more anger.

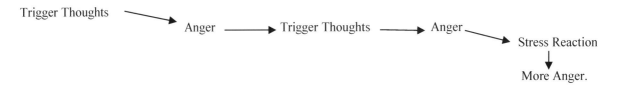

Here's an example for *anger cycle #2*:
Arturo wonders if his wife will work late at the office again tonight. He imagines himself sitting alone through the news and TV shows waiting to hear her key in the door. These thoughts trigger a sense of loneliness. He thinks the pain is her fault and converts his stressful feelings to anger. This stirs up more Trigger Thoughts as he tells himself, "She doesn't really care."

Other sources that may trigger your anger include *biases*. For example, you may favor certain types of inputs or interpretations of events over others. A bias leads you to interpret an event as aversive or negative. Thus you may perceive an accidental bump in the school hallway as premeditated. This kind of appraisal system makes too much of provoking events, triggering anger.

Another common bias is: "If you provoke me, it is OK for me to strike back." This type of thinking sets the stage for retaliation. A final type of misappraisal system can be called the "knuckle bias." As one adolescent put it, "The only thing they'll understand is a fist in the face." This kind of bias leads you to believe that aggressive force is the only option that has any meaningful effect. Many people today think that violence is an acceptable way to settle disputes.

Irrational Beliefs

While biases affect how input is weighed, generalized beliefs that you may hold will see provoking input even when there is no intentional provocation. You may think that people must or should act in a certain way and when they fail to meet these standards, you get angry. (McKay et al., 1988)

Common anger-inducing beliefs include:
- Because I want it, I should get it (entitlement). "They should appreciate my work." "I should get . . ."
- It has to be fair. "Since I worked as hard as she did, I should . . ."
- I have to be right (self-righteousness). "No, it's not that way, it's . . ." "I just don't think that's right."
- "If you cared about me, you . . ." (conditional assumption). "If I was important to you, you'd . . ." "If you were my friend, you'd . . ."
- I have to be in control. (This frequently underlies jealousy.) "Are you going out dressed that way?" "I'm not leaving until you . . ."
(Gintner, 1995, p. 9.)

The important aspect about irrational beliefs is that you really believe there is a good reason for getting upset. You feel threatened and fear that something awful may happen, even when the event is minor. Or you may be dealing with low self-esteem, which can cause an overreaction to events.

Impulsivity is frequently attributed to an underdeveloped defensive system. This is seen in adolescence more often than in mature adults. Defenses like sublimation (which refocuses energy into positive behavior) or rationalization (which constructs a logical justification for someone's actions) are unavailable for delaying an anger response. The impulsive person rarely quells a horrible urge by a rationalization such as "He's probably having a bad day." Rather, immature defenses such as fantasy, denial, or acting out are the major emotional regulators. Anger explosions operate like a release valve so that "you act it out" instead of "thinking it out."

Skill deficits in cognitive and behavioral areas contribute to an impulsive acting out of anger. There are ways to avoid or escape this. One way is using self-talk to guide behavior and delay responses (for example, "Wait a minute--hitting won't help right now. Take a breather").
Those with poor self-control are characterized by hot self-talk: "He thinks he can bully me . . ." Or the person ruminates about events, allowing the anger to build internally. Those with healthy self-talk think, "I'm not going to think about that now. I'm going to get some work done." or entertain alternative solutions to provocation such as problem-solving.

Substance use: This addictive/obsessive behavior has a disinhibiting effect on anger and on aggression. Thus the person speaks or acts in ways that normally he/she would not even consider.

Family: An aggressive individual typically comes out of a home environment characterized by high overt conflict and low levels of positive interchanges.

Stress--current life situations: Living under conditions of chronic stress, or frequent daily hassles, takes a toll on an individual's coping resources.
A major stressful life event (such as divorce or death) on top of chronic stress (such as harsh economic conditions and unemployment) can lead to an aggressive overreaction. Example: marital discord resulting in child abuse.
Consider media reports of those who go on a murder spree after a job loss or marital separation. Who or what is responsible? The person who is angry and acts out his/her anger is responsible.

What Happens in the Process of Anger?
When someone hurts us physically or emotionally we become angry. We may flare up immediately or think about it awhile and then become angry. Something happens when we are frustrated: someone or something prevents us from reaching a goal. The anger covers up our feelings of disappointment or failure. In the short run it may keep us going. In the long run it will deplete our emotional energy. Poor self-concept, negative self-evaluations and fear lie behind the anger.

Dr. Paul Hauck outlines six levels of thought people move through in getting angry:
1. "I want something."
2. "I didn't get what I wanted and am frustrated."
3. "It is awful and terrible not to get what I want."
4. "You shouldn't frustrate me! I must have my way."
5. "You're bad for frustrating me."
6. "Bad people ought to be punished."

Apply these steps to a recent episode in which you became angry. Our perception of truth begins to break down in level 3. We don't like to be frustrated, but being frustrated is not as terrible as we think. Levels 4-6 show a retreat to irrationality and can result in uncontrolled anger as we think these unhealthy thoughts.

Why must we have our way? Who says people are bad just because they frustrate us? Who says bad people ought to be punished? What is involved at the level of thought when anger goes bad? Cognitive distortions; irrational beliefs; false beliefs about spiritual truth, what is good for us, and how we can or cannot secure significance.

Anger is a great force. If you control it- it can be transmuted into a power which can move the whole world. William Shenstone

Questions:

1. How would you describe anger? What happened recently to cause anger between you and your partner?

_____

_____

_____

2. What are some sources of and triggers for anger described in the book? Which apply to you?

_____

_____

_____

3. What happens in the process of anger according to the book?

_____

_____

_____

4. When can anger be helpful according to the book? Do you agree or disagree?

_____

_____

_____

5. When can anger be harmful according to the authors? Would you add any harmful effects to the list? How has your anger harmed your relationship and life?

_____

_____

_____

6. Who is responsible for getting angry? Do you tend to blame your partner for your anger?

_____

_____

7. Check which of the following signs of problem anger apply to you (write out an example or two of how it has disturbed your relationship describing the signs and symptoms of your anger):
        1. it is too frequent. ___
        2. it is too intense. ___
        3. it lasts too long. ___
        4. it leads to aggression. ___
        5. it disturbs work or relationships. ___

8. Take the following Irrational Belief Inventory. Check which belief(s) applies to you:

I regularly think:

      ___Because I want it, I should get it (entitlement). "They should appreciate my work." "I should get . . ."
      ___It has to be fair. "Since I worked as hard as she did, I should .. ."
      ___I have to be right (self-righteousness). "No, it's not that way, it's . . ." "I just don't think that's right."
      ___"If you cared about me, you . . ." (conditional assumption). "If I was important to you, you'd . . ." "If you were my friend, you'd . . ."
      ___I have to be in control. (This frequently underlies jealousy.) "Are you going out dressed that way?" "I'm not leaving until you . . ."   (Gintner, 1995)

Which belief(s) do you struggle with? How much do these beliefs inhibit anger control?
_____
_____

9. What might you be doing to contribute to your anger? Do you have irrational beliefs, "cognitive triggers, biases, skill deficits? Do you use drugs or alcohol? Is your life overloaded with stress?
_____
_____
_____

Review the Anger Survey:
a. In what kinds of situations do you find yourself getting angry with your partner?
_____
_____
_____

b. How has anger been a problem for you and your spouse or partner? With what effects?
_____
_____
_____

c. What triggers led to feelings of anger/frustration? How did your partner trigger your anger?

_____
_____
_____

d. From the General Provocation Scenario in the book -- answer:
What lies beneath your anger? Jealousy? Disappointments? Fear? Sadness? Low self-esteem? Failure? Frustrated goals? What feelings/hurts might lie beneath your partner's anger?

_____
_____
_____
_____
_____

Foundational Insights:
"Anger is a response to fear, helplessness, frustrated goals, tense or difficult situations, false beliefs, conflicts or stress. Triggers can increase an angry response. But, when the situation or event is analyzed – one should determine whether there is a legitimate reason for getting angry. Maybe it is: "I don't like the decision that was made because_____." Or "I felt disrespected or misjudged by the way I was treated." The key is to identify the issue and decide whether it is valid. Then, approach the situation -- your partner or the other person -- to work through the matter in a healthy way."

Questions: (discuss these with your partner*)
1. What do these insights and principles teach you about the causes and triggers for anger?

_____
_____
_____

2. What is the most important aspect of these insights? How can these insights motivate you to improve your response to anger and your relationship?

_____
_____
_____

3. When have you approached provoking situations in a healthy way with your partner? Ask your spouse for an example of how you refrained from anger recently. What resulted?

_____
_____
_____

*please refrain from any negative or blaming comments. Take responsibility and only talk about yourself.

What if Question:

What if you are at home and your partner starts 'getting in your face' about not cleaning the house or finishing a project?

Your anger quotient is: 1-10 (1=low; 5= moderate; 10=high) _____
What are any triggers?

_____
_____

Your response is:

_____
_____
_____

What's good about your response (thoughts, behavior)?

_____
_____

Describe the consequences of your response:

_____
_____

How does this help you achieve your personal or relationship goals?

_____
_____

What do you need to change?

_____
_____

Lesson Three What IS Good About Anger?

> **Goal**: To learn how anger can be expressed in healthy ways to achieve your goals.

There is good anger. It is anger governed by self-control, motivated by compassion, desiring what is right versus what is wrong.

Lynette Hoy

Do you struggle with the question, "How can anything good come from anger?" You are not alone. While there are plenty of examples of harmful anger, we rarely encounter good examples. How many times this week did you get angry? Highlight the kind of behavior that resulted:

- yelling.
- rude or obscene remarks.
- aggression, violence.
- depression, hidden anger.
- other_____

What were the consequences? Highlight the attitudes or consequences that resulted:

- sense of guilt, regret, or shame.
- defensiveness or thinking, "They deserved it."
- more anger, resentment.
- broken relationships.
- trouble with the law or your employer.

The premise of this book is that feelings of anger are normal and at times justified. The degree to which you become angry, the reasons for your anger, and the outcome of your anger determine whether your anger is, in fact, good. When anger is expressed in healthy ways, it is a change agent. Anger can actually change a passive victim into someone who is confident and assertive. An aggressive person can learn self-control. Anger can motivate people to solve problems and resolve conflict.

Your anger can be converted into forgiveness versus internalized as resentment.

But when anger is hidden and suppressed, it most likely will result in depression. The tendency for many religious people and leaders is to avoid the expression of anger because they believe anger is wrong in any situation. Thus anger is viewed negatively and is often denied.

In the following situation Bob writes about his struggles with anger and control:

"My anger always stayed in check at work. One day I was tested beyond imagination by a co-worker who was trying to pick a fight over who was right regarding some technical issue. This was many years ago, but it has never left me. I allowed someone of inferior intellect to gain control over me by losing my temper and yelling (in the middle of the laboratory . . . a very academic and disciplined environment). The ironic point is that my faulty thinking said anger equals control, and by getting angry I gave up that one thing in my mind that was worth fighting for: control. The biggest cost is the alienation that follows. It isolates me from the very people to whom I want to be close. Instead of control, I gained loneliness."

Bob didn't get what he wanted. He also lost the respect and trust of his co-workers.

So, what is good about anger? Anger:
- gives you information about yourself, events, and people.
- helps energize you for action and faith.
- moves you to express your feelings and resolve conflict.
- enables you to assert yourself and move toward problem-solving.

What are some sensible, healthy admonitions for being "good and angry?"
1. Be angry, but put limitations on its expression in order to prevent harming yourself or others.
2. Take responsibility for your anger. Don't blame it on someone else.
3. Slow your anger down. Think through anger versus immediately acting it out. [1]
4. Don't let your anger intensify, as it will generally bring about harm.
5. Don't associate with angry people. [2]
6. Seek healthy resolution to issues.
7. Always consider the outcome of anger and how it will impact others as well as yourself.
8. Learn healthy ways to express your anger.

Here's How You Can Handle Someone Else's Anger-
We tend to get angry at someone who is angry. Why is that? We react defensively to angry people because we think their anger is wrong and threatening. What can we do to drain the anger from our spouse or someone else versus provoking their anger even more?

King Solomon wrote, "a gentle answer turns away wrath, but a harsh word stirs up anger." [3]
A simple method of paraphrasing what an angry person says to you can help defuse his/her anger.

Here's an example:
Angry person: "I can't stand the stress of you interrupting me when I am working on a project. You are so inconsiderate!"
You say, "You find it very stressful when I interrupt you during an important project."
Angry person: "Yes! And furthermore, I need more peace and quiet around here."
You say, "You would like more peace and want me to stop interrupting you."
Angry person: "Yes. You seem to have gotten the message."
You say, "I appreciate you sharing this with me. In the future, I will try to avoid interrupting you when I see you concentrating on a project."
At a later time when the person's anger has subsided, bring up the other issues that need resolution by saying, "When would be a good time for me to discuss my questions and concerns with you in the future?" and/or "I would like you to clarify what you meant by your need for more peace and quiet."

This example of paraphrasing should generally be used for the purpose of defusing and draining someone else's anger. It is not sufficient for use in cases where you need to work through a conflict with someone or deal with an unfair accusation or an abusive situation.

The premise of this book is to teach you that anger is good when turned into:
- Faith: Trusting in your Higher Power.
- Assertiveness: Speaking the truth in love.
- Problem-solving: Seeking the best solution.
- Conflict resolution: Negotiating to win-win.
- Forgiveness: Letting go of resentment.

What's in it for you?
What will you get out of controlling your anger? First of all, you will gain self-control and a sense of "personal power" (not power over others). No one will be able to make you angry or pull your strings. You will have the power to choose to be angry or not! Having "personal power" is pulling your own strings and gaining control over yourself. If you can keep cool, you are more likely to respond in ways that serve your best interests.
Look at the pros and cons of reacting to provocation with aggression. What are the positives and negatives?
If someone calls you a name and you hit him/her, you believe "they'll think twice about messing with me."
On the other hand, you may get sued or arrested for assault and battery. When you avoid responding aggressively, you gain self-respect and, most likely, respect from others. You also avoid negative consequences with the law.

There is such a thing as good anger. It is anger governed by self-control, motivated by compassion, desiring what is right versus what is wrong. Lynette Hoy

Questions:
1. Describe what this chapter means to you. In other words, *what is good about anger* and does this make sense to you? Can you envision experiencing good anger in your relationship?

_____

_____

_____

2. How did Bob's anger get out of control at work? What were the consequences of his anger? Can you identify with Bob? How did it affect his relationships?

_____

_____

_____

3. State in your own words some of the admonitions for being "good and angry".

_____

_____

4. How can you handle your spouse's anger according to this chapter? Do you agree with the suggested steps?

_____

_____

_____

_____

5. Describe a situation when your partner was angry and how you responded:

_____

_____

_____

6. What could you have done differently to help defuse his/her anger?

_____

_____

_____

7. Did you know that the Good Book says, "the righteous shall walk by faith"? Would you like to consider how faith might impact your expression of anger?

_____

_____

_____

Foundational Insights: *When we step back and assess the situations which cause us to feel angry – we can plan for a healthy response. When we consider the consequences of our response and the best interests of others (our partner) and ourselves – we are motivated to express anger effectively and appropriately.*

8. Describe the pros and cons for controlling your anger. How will controlling your anger positively affect your partner? How might controlling your anger affect you positively?

_____

_____

_____

_____

9. What is meant by "personal power" in the book? What will you gain *from pulling your own strings*? How will this impact your partner?

_____

_____

_____

_____

_____

10. List three anger-provoking situations you would like to handle with more self-control and wisdom. Discuss with your partner what you plan to do differently. Ask him/her for feedback*:

1. _____

_____

_____

2. _____

_____

_____

3. _____

_____

*please refrain from any negative or blaming comments.

Couple's time:

1. Share what you have learned from this lesson with your partner.

_____

_____

_____

2. What impacted you the most?

_____

_____

_____

3. Describe a time when you both handled a conflict effectively, with respect – keeping your anger under control:

_____

_____

_____

4. What benefits can result from good anger? Discuss the examples given in the book.

_____

_____

_____

_____

5. Describe what this lesson means to you. In other words, *what is good about anger* and does this make sense to you?

_____

_____

What if Question:

What if your spouse or partner interrupts you when you are trying to explain something very important?

Your anger quotient is: 1-10 (1=low; 5= moderate; 10=high) _____

Your response is:

_____

_____

_____

What's good about your response (thoughts, behavior)?

_____

_____

Describe the consequences of your response:

_____

_____

How does this help you achieve your personal or relationship goals?

_____

_____

What do you need to change? How could you respond with love and respect?

_____

_____

Lesson Four *Defusing Anger by Managing Stress*

> **Goal:** *Identify and reduce stressors in order to enhance anger management.*

> *There are very few certainties that touch us all in this mortal experience, but one of the absolutes is that we will experience hardship and stress at some point.*
>
> Dr. James Dobson

What role does stress play in anger escalation? Research has demonstrated that high stress levels precipitate angry outbursts and aggression. Take the stress inventory at the end of this lesson to learn how stress is impacting your life and emotions.

Overview of Stress: The Wikipedia Encyclopedia states that "Stress (roughly the opposite of relaxation) is a medical term for a wide range of strong external stimuli, both physiological and psychological, which can cause a physiological response called the general adaptation syndrome, first described in 1936 by Hans Selye in the Journal of Nature."

Stress and its effects

Selye was able to separate the physical effects of stress from other physical symptoms suffered by patients through his research. He observed that patients suffered physical effects not caused directly by their disease or by their medical condition.

Selye described the general adaptation syndrome as having three stages:
- alarm reaction, where the body detects the external stimulus.
- adaptation, where the body engages defensive countermeasures against the stressor.
- exhaustion, where the body begins to run out of defenses.

There are two types of stress: eustress ("positive stress") and distress ("negative stress"), roughly meaning challenge and overload.

Both types may be the result of negative or positive events. If a person both wins the lottery and has a beloved relative die on the same day, one event does not cancel the other--both are stressful events. Eustress is essential to life, like exercise to a muscle; however, distress can cause disease. (Note that what causes distress for one person may cause eustress for another, depending upon each individual's life perception.) When the word stress is used alone, typically it is referring to distress. Serenity is defined as a state in which an individual is disposition-free or largely free from the negative effects of stress, and in some cultures it is considered a state that can be cultivated by various practices, such as meditation and other forms of training. Stress can directly and indirectly contribute to general or specific disorders of body and mind. Stress can have a major impact on the physical functioning of the human body. Such stress raises the level of adrenaline and corticosterone in the body, which in turn increases the heart rate, respiration, and blood pressure and puts more physical stress on bodily organs. Long-term stress can be a contributing factor in heart failure, high blood pressure, stroke and other illnesses.

Stress is a threat to the safety and well-being of the body. In time past, the physical stress response was a means of survival: it prepared us for fight or flight. What is this so-called fight or flight reaction? It is instinctive and consists of messages sent all over the body to and from the brain. These messages alert the body of a perceived threat. In a threatening situation, we are given two options: either we can stand our ground and fight the threat or we can run away from it. The choice is made based on our perception of the situation: if we feel we have a chance of overcoming the danger (e.g., winning the fight) or not.

The various triggers for anger covered earlier are also triggers for a stress response. A stress reaction can precipitate or coincide with an angry response. Thus, avoiding triggers such as drinking, substance abuse, hot self-talk, irrational beliefs, distorted thoughts, overspending, unhealthy behavior, and any preventable stressful situations can thwart angry responses. Obviously, there are stressful circumstances in life that cannot be avoided.

Changing what you say to yourself and how you view life can greatly impact how you manage stress and anger. Your self-talk originates from your view of life and yourself. If you view life as "grab for all the gusto you can get!" based on the premise that "eat, drink, and be merry, for tomorrow we die," then you will experience more stress and anger! Why? Because you will hurry through life looking for satisfaction in anything without thinking about the consequences or caring about what is best for your life and those you love. And you will experience dissatisfaction--the opposite of what you really want! If you view life as meaningless, you will tell yourself, "what's the point?" or "why bother?" when you face responsibilities and decisions. Or if you view life as overwhelming or yourself as never measuring up, you will tell yourself, "I can't handle that" or "This is too much for me" or "I'll just fail anyway." Your negative self-talk will generate more feelings of stress, hopelessness, and less motivation for change. We call this inner talk "stress-talk." Stress-talk will cause more anger and frustration in your life. The lessons on cognitive distortions can help you challenge and change any stress-talk.

Other internal stress-talk messages occur when you try to control people. You may say to yourself, "He/she should do it my way" or "Why is she going out dressed that way?" because of your need to control. Underlying your need to control may be feelings of insecurity, jealousy, low self-worth, or the urge to teach others how to live their lives. Whatever the cause, your need for control will increase your feelings of stress and anger.

How can you deal with the need to control? First, consider these negative consequences:
- You will run out of energy and feel more frustration when you try to control everything and everyone in your life.
- You will push your family and friends away from you. No one likes a controller.
- Generally, you won't get what you want when you try to control.
- In the long-run, your inner needs of security and significance won't be met.

Complete the Am I a Controller? inventory at the end of this lesson to see if you have this tendency.

Another form of stress-talk is blaming. You may be blaming others for your anger and disappointments in life, thinking, "if they would meet my needs I would be happy." The fact is that no one will completely meet your needs and that you have the power to make choices that will help fulfill your needs. You can take ownership of your feelings and better communicate your needs by saying to others:

"I feel angry (frustrated, disappointed, overwhelmed, hurt, or let down, etc.) when
you don't listen to me (or interrupt me)."

This formula for communication helps you express your reaction and emotions without blaming. It brings up the issue and helps the other person feel less defensive. Think about some situations when you could have used this formula:

> Situation:
> I felt angry when I thought:
> Identify the issue: Was it valid? Could you have made a request?

Balance your relationships and life in order to manage stress. We were made to connect with people. Having healthy, caring, significant relationships with others gives us meaning for living, encouragement, and companionship throughout our lives.

If you are in relationships that are unhealthy because you are giving more than getting or there is too much conflict and friction, then you will feel stressed out. It could be that you tend to be codependent and need boundaries or more assertiveness in your relationships.

What about focusing on your needs and preventing negative consequences? When you engage in activities that are unhealthy it increases stress and anger. You may think that you are managing your stress by drinking, smoking, or using other substances when actually these habits are making your life miserable. Substance abuse increases irritability and is a trigger for anger.

You need to decide what to change and how to make healthy choices that will improve your health, mind, emotions, spirit, and relationships. You may find comfort in the use of substances, but it will only be temporary. The long-term negative consequences will outweigh the short-term experience and increase feelings of anger.

How can you increase the eustress (positive stress) in your life?

Take a look at your life to see how you can get revitalized. Do you have some activities that encourage and inspire you such as exercise, singing, playing an instrument, going to church, involvement in a support group, or something else meaningful or creative?

Beginning a new goal such as a class or a hobby or sport will revitalize you. What past activities would you like to reestablish? Riding your bike? Going fishing? Taking an art class? Going hiking or canoeing? These kinds of activities will create "positive stress" and refresh you! Examine your personal pace of life. See what you might need to change. Simplify your life by starting to do and be that for which you were designed. You will begin to feel more hopeful, more peaceful and encouraged as you renew your whole person, soul, and spirit. Write out new goals for your life that will include the positive activities mentioned. Begin to do one or two activities daily that will help enrich you physically, emotionally, and spiritually. If you are interested in reading more about how faith affects anger, order the first edition of What's Good About Anger? or the DVD at: www.whatsgoodaboutanger.com

Progressive Relaxation

It has been proven that relaxation techniques are beneficial for reducing stress in your life and thus decreasing the resulting feelings of anger and frustration. With so many things to do, it's easy to put off taking time to relax each day. But in doing so, you miss out on the health benefits of relaxation. Relaxation can improve how your body responds to stress by:

- Slowing your heart rate, meaning less work for your heart.
- Reducing blood pressure.
- Slowing your breathing rate.
- Reducing the need for oxygen.
- Increasing blood flow to the major muscles.
- Lessening muscle tension.

After practicing relaxation skills, you may experience these benefits:

- Fewer symptoms of illness, such as headaches, nausea, diarrhea, and pain.
- Few emotional responses such as anger, crying, anxiety, apprehension, and frustration.
- More energy.
- Improved concentration.
- Greater ability to handle problems.
- More efficiency in daily activities.

Relaxed breathing

Have you ever noticed how you breathe when you're stressed? Stress typically causes rapid, shallow breathing. This kind of breathing sustains other aspects of the stress response, such as rapid heart rate and perspiration. If you can get control of your breathing, the spiraling effects of acute stress will automatically become less intense. Relaxed breathing, also called diaphragmatic breathing, can help you.

Practice this basic technique twice a day, every day, whenever you feel tense. Follow these steps:

1. Inhale. With your mouth closed and your shoulders relaxed, inhale as slowly and deeply as you can to the count of six. As you do that, push your stomach out. Allow the air to fill your diaphragm.
2. Hold. Keep the air in your lungs as you slowly count to four.
3. Exhale. Release the air through your mouth as you slowly count to six.
4. Repeat. Complete the inhale-hold-exhale cycle three to five times.

Recommended Relaxation Technique:

Experts say it's best to practice relaxation for at least twenty minutes per day. At first, practicing the following relaxation technique may seem awkward. In time, and with practice, you'll feel more comfortable with the practice and the results. Learning to relax can help prevent the escalation of anger.

Find a quiet place where you won't be disturbed. Make sure you're sitting comfortably with your back straight or lying comfortably with your arms along your sides. Close your eyes and begin focusing on your body. Slowly breathe in through your nose and out through your mouth. When thoughts and images arise in your mind, acknowledge them, and then let them go away as you bring your focus back to your breathing. Fully experience each exhale. Practice this for about five minutes or so.

Shift your focus to your body. Start with your feet. Tighten the muscles in your feet and toes, hold them tense for a couple seconds, then release the tension and let your feet relax. Next, focus on your calves. Tighten the muscles in your calves, hold them tense for a couple seconds, then release the tension and let your calves relax.

Repeat this through all of your major muscle groups as you move your attention up your body. Tense your thighs, hold, and then relax.

Move to your chest, hands, arms, shoulders, and finally your face.

After you have relaxed all of your muscle groups, mentally check over your body from head to toe and feel for any muscles that are still tense. If you notice a part of you that is not totally relaxed, tense it up a little, hold, and then relax. Sit, or lay, in silence with your eyes closed for twenty minutes or for as long as is comfortable.

Many people incorporate prayer during their time of relaxation.

Questions:
1. Define stress. What are the two different types?

_____

_____

2. How has stress affected your life and your ability to manage anger in your relationship?

_____

_____

Foundational insights:

Making personal choices to live a healthy life-style can decrease the stress which precipitates anger. Learning relaxation techniques can slow down your physiological "fight-flight" response to anger.

Questions: After writing out your answers – discuss questions 1-5 with your partner.
1. What kinds of activities or situations cause you to feel stressed out?

_____

_____

2. How has stress affected you personally or relationally?

_____

_____

3. What kinds of "stress-talk" do you experience? How can you challenge or change these inner messages? How do these internal messages affect your relationship and view of your partner?

_____

_____

_____

4. Which stress management techniques will help change the triggers and provoking situations in your life and thus, decrease anger escalation? Have you tried any?

_____
_____
_____

5. If stress management is so important to anger management - how can you develop it? Review and use the Relaxation exercises. Try the relaxation exercise together.

_____
_____
_____

6. Which causes for stress in your life do you have control over?

_____
_____
_____

7. Complete this question individually: Do you struggle with blaming or controlling others? (take the Do You Fit the Description of a Controller or Abuser? Inventory) Do you see this as a problem? How can you change that tendency? How do you specifically try to control your partner?

_____
_____
_____

8. What are you planning to do to increase the "eustress" in your life? How can you increase "eustress" activities in your marriage?

_____
_____

What if Question:
What if your spouse is stressed out by the kids arguing or the neighbors yelling? How can you help defuse the stress?

Your anger quotient is: 1-10 (1=low; 5= moderate; 10=high) _____

Your response is:

_____
_____
_____

What's good about your response (thoughts, behavior)?

_____
_____

Describe the consequences of your response:

_____

_____

How does this help you achieve your personal or relationship goals?

_____

_____

What do you need to change? How could applying the stress management skills help your response?

_____

_____

Do You Fit the Description of a Controller or Abuser? Answer these questions honestly:
Do you ever:

____ Embarrass, make sarcastic remarks or fun of your spouse/partner in front of your friends or family?

____ Put down your spouse's accomplishments or goals? Demonstrate extreme jealousy?

____ Make your spouse feel unable to make decisions? Yell at her/him, let your temper get out of control?

____ Use intimidation or threats to gain compliance from him/her? Tell him/her that he/she is nothing without you?

____ Treat him/her roughly -- grab, push, pinch, shove, or hit him/her?

____ Call her/him several times a night or show up to make sure she/he is where she/he said she/he would be?

____ Use drugs or alcohol as an excuse for saying hurtful things or abusing her/him?

____ Blame her/him for how you feel or act?

____ Pressure him/her sexually for things he/she isn't ready for? Show cruelty to animals?

____ Make her/him feel like there is "no way out" of the relationship?

____ Prevent her/him from doing things she wants--like spending time with her/him friends or family?

____ Try to keep her/him from leaving after a fight or leave her/him somewhere after a fight to "teach her/him a lesson"?

Do you almost always need (with your partner):

____ To have things done your way?

____ To have the last word?

____ To make your point understood?

____ To behave negatively (yell, use obscenities, put-downs, or name calling or force) when you don't get your way?

____ To behave negatively when you feel misunderstood?

____ To demonstrate how right you are?

____ To show how wrong your partner is?

____ To have your wishes granted?

____ To react negatively when your partner disappoints you?

____ To respond with an outburst of anger when your partner misunderstands or disappoints you?

Do you cause your partner to:

____ Sometimes feel scared of you because you make threatening gestures or indirect threats or throw or break objects?

____ Make excuses for your behavior?

____ Believe that he/she is the only one who needs to change, not you?

___ Avoid conflict and never disagree with you in order to "keep the peace"?

___ Feel like no matter what he/she does, he/she can't please you?

___ Placate you by doing whatever you want and rarely doing what he/she wants?

___ Stay with you because he/she is afraid of the consequences of leaving you?

If you have checked any of these symptoms, you have the characteristics of a controller. If you checked any of these symptoms--physical, sexual abuse, verbal threats, outbursts or rageful behavior, harassment, manipulation by fear, cruelty to animals--you fit the description of a batterer and abuser with severe anger and control issues. You need help.

Explore these questions and challenge yourself: What makes you need to force your partner to grant your every wish and expectation? You need to explore what is driving you to control and/or batter your spouse. Call a professional counselor. Contact a local domestic violence agency for Batterer's Intervention classes (in the USA, National Domestic Violence Agency at 1-800-799-7233).

For more resources visit www.counselcareconnection.org and www.whatsgoodaboutanger.com

THE STRESS OF ADJUSTING TO CHANGE

EVENTS	SCALE OF IMPACT
Death of a spouse	100
Divorce	73
Marital separation	65
Jail term	63
Death of close family member	63
Personal injury or illness	53
Marriage	50
Fired at work	47
Marital reconciliation	45
Retirement	45
Change in health of family member	44
Pregnancy	40
Sex difficulties	39
Gain of new family member	39
Business readjustment	39
Change in financial state	38
Death of close friend	37
Change to different line of work	36
Change in number of arguments with spouse	35
Mortgage over $200,000	31
Foreclosure of mortgage or loan	30
Change in responsibilities at work	29
Son or daughter leaving home	29
Trouble with in-laws	29
Outstanding personal achievement	28
Wife begins or stops work	26
Begin or end school	26
Change in living conditions	25
Revision of personal habits	24
Trouble with boss	23
Change in work hours or conditions	20
Change in residence	20
Change in schools	20
Change in recreation	19
Change in church activities	19
Change in social activities	18
Mortgage or loan (mod-high)	17
Change in sleeping habits	16
Change in number of family gatherings	15
Change in eating habits	15
Vacation	13
Christmas	12
Minor violations of the law	11

Total Score: ____

Determine which life events have occurred in your life over the past two years and add up your total stress score. If your total score is under 150, you are less likely to be suffering the effects of cumulative stress. If it is between 150 and 300, you may be suffering from chronic stress, depending on how you perceived and coped with the particular life events that occurred. If your score is over 300, it is likely you are experiencing some detrimental effects of cumulative stress. Please note that the degree to which any particular event is stressful to you will depend on how you perceive it. ***Resource: 1967, by Pergamon Press, Inc***

Lesson Five *Handling Anger Effectively*

Goal: *To learn how to process anger and frustration through healthy communication and problem-solving skills.*

Anyone can become angry. That is easy. But to be angry with the right person, to the right degree, at the right time, for the right purpose and in the right way – that is not easy.

Aristotle

When you are overcome with anger, you may think it's impossible to have self-control.

Let's take a look at some examples of people who experienced being "good and angry." Bob wrote the following in answer to the question, "How did you recently control your anger?"

"I stopped the cycle. When I missed seeing the trigger setup early enough to just avoid the trap, I still know what I feel like when I am starting to get angry. When I start to feel even a little like that, I just call for a time-out or I pause and remind myself of how important it is to remain in control of myself, not my spouse or the other person.

"Recently I was having an emotionally charged discussion with my spouse. This of course means that we both felt strongly about the topic and had opposing viewpoints. I was able to look ahead and see how the conversation was going to unfold, so I stopped talking.

I started asking questions to understand her viewpoint. This is much easier to do when I remind myself that she is not trying to hurt me, she really loves me, and she wants the best for both of us. It's amazing what some corrected thinking can accomplish."

Notice how Bob applies a time-out, uses clarifying questions, corrects his thinking, and considers the potential escalation. He also "thinks the best" vs. "the worst" of his spouse's motives. These steps, perspective and skills keep anger and conflict from escalating. This is a healthy example of how to work through anger.

Many centuries ago a righteous man named Nehemiah wrote about an incident when he became angry: "I was very angry when I heard their outcry and these words. I took counsel with myself, and I brought charges against the nobles and the officials. I said to them, 'You are exacting interest, each from his brother.' And I held a great assembly against them." [1]

Nehemiah felt "very angry" when he heard about his country-men's dilemma (they were being exploited by the rich). He took time out to ponder the situation and how to approach it. He then went on to confront the nobles and officials. We see here that not all anger is wrong; there is a righteous anger, and it would be wrong not to act on it. As Aristotle said, "Anyone can become angry. That is easy. But to be angry with the right person, to the right degree, at the right time, for the right purpose and in the right way--that is not easy." What is the right way to handle anger? Here are some steps to consider.

Initial Awareness of Hurt or Anger
Too often we become extremely angry before we even recognize that we are angry.
Early awareness is key. What are the elements of such early awareness?

1. Recognize the underlying feelings of tension, sadness, fear, frustration, hurt, rejection, etc.
2. Take time out to reflect. Be "slow to anger.' [2]
3. Many find it helpful to pray about the problem, seeking spiritual help and guidance.
4. Identify the issue. Decide whether you are distorting the truth about the event or person. What are you angry about?
What did the other person do that hurt or frustrated you? Think about the behavior that bothered you. Don't make judgments about others' motives.
5. Evaluate whether the issue is valid. Ask, "Do I have the right to be angry?" Sometimes we do, but sometimes we don't.
6. Address the issue/problem, and express your feelings: "I was frustrated/hurt/angry when you forgot about our appointment."
How are we to go about doing this?
• Establish a plan of action: "I would like to request that you call me the next time you are going to be late."
• Provide options for change: "Please take a time-out when you begin to get angry." "Please treat me with respect."
• Negotiate a resolution: "What do you want to do about disciplining the children?"
• Plan a time-frame: "I would like to see changes made over the next month."
• Express how you will help the situation: "I will call a time-out if I think the conflict is getting too hot." "I will make my requests respectfully rather than nagging you in the future."
Learn to handle your anger with assertiveness (see the lesson on Anger and Assertiveness).
7. Get guidance from a pastor, counselor, or trustworthy confidantc.
8. Put the issue in perspective. Ask yourself: "Is this issue really worth getting upset over and worth bringing up? Or can I let go of it in light of the fact that I may have misunderstood the person? Or maybe the issue/situation is just not that important and I can overlook it."
9. Forgive and forget. Forgiveness brings resolution and is a step toward reconciliation.

Problem-solving

Anger is a result of feeling that you are helpless in a given situation. You can't solve the problem. The problem is too big, overwhelming, or painful. Difficulties come in all sizes and shapes, and you seem to be having more than your fair share.

You may ask, "Why is life so difficult and hard? And why do some people seem to have it easy?"

Establish a plan of action. Write out options and solutions that will help you resolve the problem.

You would do well to consider the following:
• What can you learn about the issue you are facing?
• What can you do about this problem? List all reasonable options, and then choose one or two.
• Try out one of the options. You can always apply another option if your first choice is not working out. Evaluate how it is affecting you and your spouse.
• How can someone help you? Ask for counsel.
• What resources are available to resolve your problem?
• What support can you ask for or make use of?

Thinking Ahead Reminders

Here are some ideas and questions to tell yourself before and during a conflict to maintain self-control:

"Keep your breathing even."

"What is it that I have to do?"

"Take it one step at a time."

"Stick to the issue and don't take it seriously."

"What's going to happen if . . ."

"Do I need to be cool so I'm not the fool?"

"Is it really worth it?" "How will this affect our relationship?"

"Will this make a difference in a week?"

"What are some helpful things I could say or do?"

(Gintner, p. 22-23).

Write these down on a 3x5 card, then review and keep them in your wallet or purse.

Questions for Thought

1. What skills and changes did Bob employ to help manage his anger when he was having an emotionally charged discussion with his spouse?

_____

_____

_____

2. How did Nehemiah express his anger about his countrymen's dilemma? How would you evaluate Nehemiah's anger according to Aristotle's principles for being "good and angry" above?

_____

_____

_____

Foundational Insights

Anger may build inside when you feel invalidated or when you are unable to impact decisions or when you are frustrated in meeting personal and family needs and goals. Your anger may be based on unrealistic expectations of someone else or even yourself or an unhealthy need to control people and events. Identifying the validity of the issue underlying your anger and your motivation is necessary to determine your plan of action or how to process the anger in effectively.

3. What are the causes of anger mentioned in this quote?

_____

_____

4. Write out the 9 steps for handling anger effectively.

_____
_____
_____
_____
_____

5. Which steps have you implemented in the past? Which steps could help prevent an angry outburst between you and your partner in the future?

_____
_____
_____

Discuss the following questions with your spouse or partner:
6. What makes each step in the process so important to managing anger and relationship conflict?

_____
_____
_____
_____

7. Talk about the steps for problem-solving and how these steps could improve your relationship:

_____
_____
_____
_____

8. How can each of you apply some of these steps when a situation provokes you to anger in the future? Write out and discuss a scenario with your spouse using the problem-solving approach.

_____
_____
_____

For personal reflection and application:
9. Which of the Thinking Ahead Reminders could help you "cool down" when facing an anger-provoking situation? Write out some of these reminders and keep them on your Iphone, IPad, and Smart Phone or in your wallet or purse.

_____
_____
_____

10. Do your angry episodes pass Aristotle's test for being "good and angry"? Why or why not?

_____
_____

What if Question:

What if you are in the car and your partner takes the wrong street causing you to be late for work?

Your anger quotient is: 1-10 (1=low; 5= moderate; 10=high) _____

Your response is:

_____

_____

_____

What's good about your response (thoughts, behavior)?

_____

_____

Describe the consequences of your response:

_____

_____

How does this help you achieve your personal and relationship goals?

_____

_____

What do you need to change? What skills could you apply from this lesson?

_____

_____

52

Lesson Six *Anger and Assertiveness*

> **Goal**: *To identify and apply ways of expressing anger and frustration through the use of assertive communication.*

Do not be angry with me if I tell you the truth.

Socrates

Assertiveness is not aggressive or passive. Assertive people express their thoughts and feelings forthrightly without getting squashed or squashing others in the process.

Some who read this book might get the impression that one should never get angry--the risk is just too great. That, of course, is not the case. There are legitimate reasons for getting angry! Sometimes we rationalize and defend why we had an outburst. Other times we may try our hardest to not ever be angry.

Having your anger under control does not mean you have to be a wallflower--or, worse, a doormat--that you never disagree with anyone, never stand up for yourself, never confront someone and tell him or her that he or she is wrong. Handling anger the right way, with self-control, does not mean that you should stuff all angry feelings and never express them or be assertive.

Many people act out their anger aggressively, thinking they are just being assertive. The truth is that assertive behavior and communication are not aggressive, as we will explain later on. You may struggle with "acting out" your anger in harmful ways and thus, are experiencing legal, work, or relationship consequences. Making the choice to control the aggression and/or verbal outbursts will take determination and application of new behaviors and better ways to communicate.

Some of you may be indirect about expressing your feelings and needs. It's important to know that good anger is often assertive--communicating reasonable requests and opinions.

Maybe you find this difficult. Perhaps as a child you were taught that it is self-centered to talk about yourself or to express your feelings. Or you may have grown up in a volatile environment where angry outbursts were the norm. Thus, you learned to react with "fits of rage" or out of fear--to hide your anger.

Which of the following describes your anger?

When I feel intense anger I have outbursts: ____

When I feel angry I lose my temper: ____

When I feel angry I tell the other person off: ____

When I feel angry I hide it and don't talk to the other person: ____

When I feel angry I use sarcasm to get my point across: ____

When I feel angry I ignore the problem but, feel resentful: ____

When I feel anger, I choose to distract myself: ____

When I feel anger, I find relief through drinking or use of substances: ____

If you have checked any of the above--learning assertive communication will help you! Take the assertiveness inventory at the end of this lesson.

You may not be direct about your opinions or disagreements because you fear people will be put off or that it will just cause a conflict. You may end up being so indirect that nearly all the time you let others speak for you. This type of communication tends to result in frustration and hidden anger.

As an indirect or passive person you may share your thoughts and feelings in a roundabout way and are apt to sound something like this: "They just laid off most of my department . . . It's kind of . . . . Well, you know. . . . But what can you do?" When you can't express your wants openly, you have to hint--"It looks like a nice day . . . our neighbors went to play tennis" or "The newspaper mentioned an arts and crafts show this Sunday"--and hope your friend or spouse will pick up on it.

You may be a person who doesn't give a hoot about what others think. You may give them the finger, shout, or threaten when they don't meet your expectations or cross you in some way. You may struggle with "hot self-talk" and come out swinging when someone provokes you.

If you are non-assertive or passive it's difficult to decide when to stand up for your "reasonable rights" and state your opinion and when to go the extra mile in considering others' interests. You may end up apologizing for someone else's mistakes. When someone spills their coffee on you, you say you're sorry for being in the wrong place. When someone puts you down, you pretend you didn't hear the remark.

In either case, for those who are aggressive or passive, assertiveness is a healthy skill you can use effectively to defuse and work through anger.

A WORKING DEFINITION OF ASSERTIVENESS

What is assertiveness? It's a way of confronting an unpleasant or difficult situation without getting squashed or squashing others in the process. When you use assertiveness you can negotiate reasonable changes by stating directly what you think, feel, and want. Assertiveness builds intimacy, solves interpersonal problems, and increases honesty, valid requests, and legitimate refusals in your relationships. Assertiveness gives you the opportunity to air your grievances and frustrations in a healthy way instead of burying them or eventually blowing up.

Assertiveness is right!

I (Ted Griffin) can testify to the power and benefit of godly assertiveness, in this case my wife's. When I was tearing my family apart with selfish, destructive anger, my wife was able, with the courage God provides, to come to the point where she could at appropriate times tell me, "I won't allow you to talk to me in that way," then end the conversation until I had cooled down. Or she would leave the house, with the kids, leaving me alone at home to consider how my anger was affecting our family. In these and other ways her gentle but firm assertiveness made me see what my anger was doing to myself and to everyone in our home. Though I didn't always like her standing up to me at the time, looking back I can see that God used it to get my attention and to help me see how I was wrong and how I needed to change.

When I (Lynette) was first married, I would shut down and give the "cold shoulder" whenever I felt hurt by my husband. This brought a great deal of distress to our relationship because he could not understand what was wrong with me. One time he said, "Our relationship is more important than any issue. We need to work this out no matter what." It was obvious that I needed to learn how to directly communicate issues and any anger I was harboring in a healthier manner. Of course, there are a number of alternatives to healthy assertiveness. You can fake your feelings, suffer silently, retreat, manipulate, or demand your way in a fit of rage. Ultimately these options are self-defeating, harmful to you and others resulting in negative consequences.

PRACTICAL STRATEGIES FOR BEING APPROPRIATELY ASSERTIVE

One of the keys to making assertiveness work for you while also making it palatable for others is to combine it with active listening. Listening involves hearing and paraphrasing back what others say to you. It gives you the opportunity to pick up on their viewpoints and continue the dialogue. You don't have to agree with their opinions, but active listening will show that you value and respect them. This will increase the likelihood that others will take time to listen to you.

Begin summarizing what people say to you with phrases such as: • "In other words . . ."
- "Let me get this straight . . ."
- "So you felt that . . ."
- "What I hear you saying is . . ."
- "If I understand you correctly . . ."
- "Would you say that . . . ?"
- "Do I understand you to mean . . . ?"

Make certain that your paraphrase is brief and includes the facts and feelings the person is expressing. Some sample paraphrases might be:
- "You were really scared when the dog ran in front of the car."
- "You feel frustrated because I missed our appointment."

When you can summarize what someone has said to you, you will clarify what they are saying and keep the dialogue from getting heated.

Still, the most difficult aspect of communication comes when you take the risk to talk about your opinions, feelings, and needs. Don't let fear or anger get in the way! Learning assertive communication skills is the next step.

Here are some examples of ways of assertiveness that will help you express your opinions, confront others, state your feelings, or make requests:
1. Stating your preference or opinion: "My preference is _____."
   "What I'd like is _____."
2. Expressing your feelings: "I feel _____ when_____."
3. Making requests: "This movie is not what I hoped it would be. I would like to leave."
4. Disagreeing with someone: "I disagree with you when you say _____."
5. Saying yes or no without making excuses: "I am unable to come to lunch."
6. Using "I" statements for confronting: "I feel_____ when you_____ because_____."

Here is an assertiveness approach you can apply when you need to bring up an issue. It's called the ASERT Model:

- Approach the person calmly and with respect.
- State the problem. Think over and state the facts of the problem.
- Express yourself. State your feelings.
- Request change and feedback. Specify one behavior change.
- Then listen to the other person's thoughts and opinions.
- Talk it out. Paraphrase the other person's ideas. Discuss the consequences, considerations, and options.

Write out recent interactions you have had with people in which you could have been less demanding or less passive. Then, using the ASERT model, rewrite the scenario using the paraphrasing and assertiveness skills.

Resolve to start trying your newly acquired skills this week:

- When your partner asks you for a favor that conflicts with your schedule, just say, "I wish I could help you, but I have another appointment."
- When your partner is rude to you, talk to them privately, asking them to treat you with respect in the future.
- When your partner is disagreeing with you on a topic - respectfully share your opinion.

Assertiveness need not be a painful exercise of skills. You can get something out of communicating more directly with others. You can direct your anger into a healthy exchange of words leading to a resolution of problems. Aristotle wrote, "Many a friendship is lost for lack of speaking." Speaking up will help you build closer relationships with others and gain more confidence in yourself! Just think -- no more hinting, raging, manipulating, forcing or demanding your way! Instead you can state your ideas, thoughts, and feelings confidently while at the same time managing your anger!

To be assertive in the ways we have been talking about is not easy. It takes wisdom (what to say and when to say it), patience, discernment, and above all courage.

Dealing with Difficult People: There are times when you will encounter people who are difficult and overbearing. Here are some suggestions for handling these situations.

1. *The broken record technique*: Rehearse making your requests in a firm but calm voice when someone does not respond to you. "I want my money back . . . just give me my money back . . . all I want is my money back . . ." It is critical to rehearse this prior to a situation in which you expect to encounter resistance and to help you maintain composure and self-control. Remember to not raise your voice.

2. When someone is engaging in annoying behavior, *"ignoring" or not reacting* may be the best course of action. Ignoring may lower the probability that it will occur again. However, this technique must be applied carefully since the other party may become more obnoxious. Ignoring includes: making no eye contact with the party and maintaining a neutral facial expression; attending to something else or the positive behaviors of the others in the room; as soon as the other party stops acting obnoxiously, attend to him/her. Use discernment when applying this skill.

3. *Fogging.* This technique is a way of confusing a provoking individual by appearing to lightheartedly agree with him or her. For example, a fogging response to someone who criticizes your clothing might be, "You really think I have no taste."

A fogging response helps you maintain control by not taking a comment seriously. It also breaks the escalation cycle by side-stepping an aggressive counter-response.

(Gintner; Feindler and Ecton)

Questions for Thought

1. Which of the following describes your anger?

When I feel intense anger I have outbursts: ____

When I feel angry I lose my temper: ____

When I feel angry I tell the other person off: ____

When I feel angry I hide it and don't talk to the other person: ____

When I feel angry I use sarcasm to get my point across: ____

When I feel angry I ignore the problem but, feel resentful: ____

When I feel anger, I choose to distract myself: ____

When I feel anger, I find relief through drinking or use of substances: ____

*If you have checked any of the above – learning assertive communication will help you!

2. How does the book describe assertiveness?

_____

_____

_____

3. How did you score on the assertiveness inventory? If you are an aggressive or volatile person when you get angry – how will learning assertive communication help your relationship?

_____

_____

Communication example: "In a cartoon from the Lockhorns - LeRoy asks Loretta what she is doing at her desk. Loretta says "I'm writing a romantic novel LeRoy and *you're not* in it"." What kind of communication is this? Loretta's way of communicating – though truthful – is harsh versus "speaking the truth in love". This is an example of sarcasm not assertiveness.

Foundational Insights:

Anger can be communicated in acceptable and even loving ways. Anger can be expressed as a request, a boundary, an opinion, a decision or a question. When you communicate anger with respect – you will have more success in resolving issues, meeting your needs and building healthy relationships with your partner.

4. How can assertiveness help you better manage anger if you are a passive person or tend to hold your feelings in or are manipulative or indirect?

_____
_____
_____

5. What kind of assertiveness (making a request, stating a boundary or opinion, preference, decision or question) have you used in the past and how did it impact your anger & relationship?

_____
_____
_____

6. Have you encountered difficult or over-bearing people? Describe the skills – broken record, ignoring, fogging – which will help you deal with these people/situations:

_____
_____
_____

Practice with partner/spouse:
7. Write out how to handle one or two situations (occurring with your partner) using the ASERT approach (in this workbook). Practice these with your spouse or partner. (use another sheet)

_____
_____

What if Question:
What if your partner wants to cancel an important event (a concert or show you love) to do something else? Or what if he/she doesn't show up for company affair that has been scheduled?

Your anger quotient is: 1-10 (1=low; 5= moderate; 10=high) _____

Your response is:

_____
_____
_____

What's good about your response (thoughts, behavior)?

_____
_____

Describe the consequences of your response:

_____
_____

How does this help you achieve your personal and relationship goals?

_____

_____

What do you need to change? How could the ASERT approach help you respond?

_____

_____

Activity: Practice using the ASERT approach in your relationship.

Assertiveness Inventory © copyright 2006 by Lynette J. Hoy, NCC, LCPC

This inventory will help you determine whether you are appropriately assertive, i.e., respectfully honest and direct about your feelings and opinions with others. Check the statements only if these are generally true of you. Be honest. This inventory may not be duplicated in any form.

When expressing myself I generally:
1. ___ have difficulty being clear and direct.
2. ___ keep quiet letting others speak.
3. ___ am abrasive or demanding.
4. ___ leave wishing I had said more.
5. ___ become too loud.
6. ___ say too much.
7. ___ clearly state how I feel or what I think.
8. ___ use active listening, tact and respect.
9. ___ ask others for their opinions after stating mine.
10. ___ tend to manipulate.
11. ___ make indirect suggestions about my feelings and thoughts.
12. ___ state my thoughts without denigrating someone's character.
13. ___ clarify what other people say.
14. ___ base my opinion on facts and behavior.
15. ___ label or stereotype others.
16. ___ consider others opinions as well as my own.
17. ___ find fault with other people.
18. ___ use a firm voice when necessary.
19. ___ use forceful gestures.
20. ___ communicate concern for others.
21. ___ quietly rationalize why I didn't speak up.
22. ___ hint about my feelings and wants.
23. ___ speak calmly and directly.
24. ___ turn conversations around to my needs and agenda.
25. ___ confront unpleasant issues directly but, with gentleness.
26. ___ when I am angry I tend to shut-down and give the "cold shoulder."
27. ___ when I am frustrated I don't hold back any of my feelings.
28. ___ I have difficulty communicating my ideas to others.

Once you have finished this inventory rate yourself as directed below.
Rate yourself as:
1. Appropriately assertive if you checked most of these:
7, 8, 9, 12, 13, 14, 16, 18, 20, 23, 25.
2. Passively pining if you checked any of these: 1, 2, 4, 21, 26, 28
3. Mostly manipulative if you checked: 10, 11, 22, 24
4. Aggressive or blaming if you checked: 3, 5, 6, 15, 17, 19, 27
5. Muddled mess: if you checked some of statements from more than one of the categories.

Lesson Seven *Managing Conflict*

> **Goal**: To identify and apply conflict resolution skills to disputes and disagreements.

I don't have to attend every argument I'm invited to.

Author Unknown

Whenever you are angry, you are dealing with conflict as well; and every time you experience real conflict, you also, at least to some extent, on some level, feel anger. Remember, not all anger is bad, and neither is all conflict.

Conflict is an inevitable part of life, work, and relationships: miscommunication between a worker and a boss; an argument between a husband and wife over finances; aggravation when a driver cuts you off or somebody at church is mad at you and refuses to speak to you. At work, what if a co-worker doesn't meet the deadline for his or her part of a combined project? How should you respond when your boss asks you to do something clearly unethical? Do you hold your tongue, wait to see what will happen, or confront, defend, maybe even blow up?

At home, what if a teenage son or daughter refuses to stop using foul language? What if a husband can't account for missing funds nearly every week but insists he has not fallen back into a gambling addiction? What if a mother refuses to let her ex-husband see their children even though the judge said he has visitation rights? If you find yourself in one of these situations, do you hold back, or do you protest, fight, and insist on your rights?

Conflict can result in either problem-solving and resolution or all-out war! How we approach conflict greatly impacts the outcome. Having the right mind-set going into it won't guarantee peaceful resolution, but having a wrong mind-set will bring certain failure and continuing tension. As long we live on earth, we will experience conflict! And that's not always bad.

GOOD REASONS TO ACCEPT AND FACE CONFLICT

• To stand against wrong. For example, if someone is taking drugs or abusing alcohol – confronting them and challenging them to get help; holding a teenage son or daughter who missed curfew accountable (or following through on the threatened consequences); going to court because you received a traffic ticket unfairly.

• To protect someone. For example, if a man is physically abusing his wife or child.

• Because the situation, realistically and practically, just can't continue the way it is. For example, your marriage won't last much longer, or your boss may soon fire you.

• Because of a clear sense of urgency or responsibility. For example, William Wilberforce's long but successful battle to end slavery in the British Empire in the nineteenth century.

• To seek and experience resolution and/or reconciliation. You're ready to make peace (to confess the ways you contributed to the conflict, forgive, negotiate), and you're pretty sure the other party is too.

• Because you know you need to make right your previous response or behavior during a conflict-to confess your faults, resolve the anger, ask forgiveness, etc.

THE IMPORTANCE OF COMPASSION WHEN FACING CONFLICT

What is compassion? It is the ability to enter into the mind and heart of another, to share his sorrow, to know him "from within," thus giving rise to mercy and understanding.

In the Revelations of Divine Love Julian of Norwich calls compassion a wound. It is so because human experience teaches us that if we love we suffer. It's therefore easier not to love, for if we do we give the other power to hurt us. The pains of those we love become our own, and the more we love the more we open ourselves to possible rejection, with its attendant emotions. If we love we "feel" for others, and the more we widen our hearts to include all, the more we shall find ourselves bearing the sorrows of the world. Elizabeth Ruth Obbard "Magnificat" pg. 47, 49-50

A definition: Compassion means feeling what the other person feels, feeling with him or her, being able to put yourself in his or her shoes, caring enough to see his or her side.

The Holy Bible tells us to "Put on . . . compassion, kindness, humility, meekness, and patience, bearing with one another and, if one has a complaint against another, forgiving each other. . . . And above all these put on love, which binds everything together in perfect harmony." [1]

When facing conflict we face three crucial choices, and our answers make all the difference.

• Relationship or winning? If the latter, sooner or later you will lose the relationship. This is not a game!
• Connect or conquer? The first is servant-hood, the second pride.
• Love or dominate? Couples often state the following at their weddings, "Love is patient and kind; love does not envy or boast; it is not arrogant or rude. It does not insist on its own way; it is not irritable or resentful." [2]

If a wrong, selfish attitude isn't put aside, the conflict will only increase.

Practical Strategies for Managing Conflict

Step 1: When you clash or disagree with another person, one way to prevent escalation is to take a time-out to consider the issues and your response. Don't feel pressured to resolve the situation immediately. Withdraw from the person, not huffily or in condescension, but with kind words to the effect, "It's probably best if we talk about this later, when we've both cooled down and have had a chance to think over what's bothering us and what we really want to say."

But don't make the time-out open-ended; try to decide when you will get back together to talk (in ten minutes? tomorrow over dinner? Wednesday night after work?). Use the time-out to pray or meditate and determine what concerns you have or what requests you might make.

Step 2: Sum up what the other person says by paraphrasing his or her demands, viewpoints, and comments. Most people don't listen well and tend to react defensively when engaged in conflict. Summarizing what someone says doesn't mean agreement with the other person's opinion or request, but it does demonstrate that you are listening, that you care and are trying to understand.

• "In other words, you were not able to get the project done on time, and you hope I can finish it for you."

• "What I hear you saying is that you feel stressed out and need me to listen to you."

Step 3: Communicate your need and viewpoint graciously yet with boundaries.

• "I was able to complete my part of the project, and wish I could help you but, I have other household responsibilities right now."

• "I want to take time to listen to you — can we talk after supper?"

Application: Write out a scenario in which you experienced conflict with your spouse. Envision how you could respond by using the time-out and sum-up skills and communicating your viewpoint.

Now do the same for a situation at work or in another setting.

Applying the sum-up skills and seeking wisdom will afford you greater opportunity for success in the workplace and in all your relationships.

Question: How can I control my anger when someone (a "downer") is unfairly blaming or judging me?

Answer: Here are some steps to take. First of all, listen attentively to what is being said. Try to understand and clarify the issue and don't defend yourself. Apply this only to your marriage.

Example:

Partner: "You didn't complete that project on time (or finish the room, house-cleaning, etc.)! You just don't care!"

You: "You think I don't care because I didn't finish the project. Did I get that right?"

Partner: "Yes! I could have finished the project myself along with everything else I am doing! "

Healing the Wounds of Anger in Marriage

You: "You think I don't care because I didn't finish the project; so you think you may as well have done it. I would like to explain to you what happened. Are you willing to listen to me?"

Partner: "Yes. But I am still so disappointed with you."

You: "Thank you for telling me your feelings. I didn't finish the project because the kids had some unexpected needs (or other responsibilities/clients at work took precedence). I know that you are disappointed but I now have time to work on the project."

Partner: "OK. But, I'm still pretty angry about this."

You (now work toward resolution: "I will do the project and have it done in a few days. I hope you can understand that I have felt stressed out too."

Questions for Thought

1. What are the causes of conflicts in your relationship? What results from your conflicts?

_____
_____
_____

2. Describe the reasons to accept and face conflict from the book:

_____
_____
_____
_____
_____
_____
_____
_____

3. What positive role can compassion play when you are facing conflict in your relationship?

_____
_____
_____

4. What does the quote: "I don't have to attend every argument I'm invited to" mean? Do you agree or disagree? Are there some arguments you could avoid or overlook with your partner?

_____
_____
_____

5. Summarize the steps in Practical Strategies for Managing Conflict. Write out a recent conflict you have experienced with your partner applying the steps to it. Discuss this with your partner.

_____
_____
_____
_____
_____
_____
_____
_____

6. What is your normal reaction when someone else unfairly accuses you of some wrong doing? Is the example in the book helpful? Why or why not?

_____
_____
_____

Foundational Insights: _Conflict is normal and a process which both parties, when willing, can work through. When conflict management skills along with compassion are applied to disputes – relationships can improve and successful resolution is possible._

Discuss this question with your partner.

7. How has your perspective on conflict changed? Which steps in conflict management would you like to apply from this lesson and chapter with your partner?

_____
_____
_____
_____
_____
_____

66

Lesson Eight Turn Your Anger into Forgiveness

Goals: *To learn that forgiveness is possible and is a vital aspect of bringing the process of anger to a conclusion.*
To practice confession and to forgive someone – especially your spouse.

Resentment is like taking poison and waiting for the other person to die.

Malachy McCourt

To forgive is to set a prisoner free and discover that the prisoner was you.

Lewis B. Smedes

It's challenging to think about forgiving people who have hurt us, isn't it? We often don't want to let go of the painful memories of abuse, put-downs, broken promises and harsh words. I (Lynette) can remember when one of my sisters refused to give me my portion of our father's inheritance. I felt hurt and angry. It was difficult to forgive her, but in time I did with the help of God. The question is--how can we unlock the door of forgiveness? First we need to understand some facts:

- Forgiveness, though difficult, is possible.
- Forgiveness is vital to resolving anger.
- Forgiveness is the road to personal healing and reconciliation with God and others.
- Forgiveness is an ongoing process.
- Forgiveness emulates the highest quality of humanity.
- Forgiveness sets you free from the past.

The Challenge of Forgiveness

Talking about forgiveness causes us to reflect on some very personal, hurtful experiences in our lives. We don't want to think about those times, and we find ourselves struggling to resolve the memories of pain and inflicted wounds by others.

What are some of the most challenging things to forgive?
People who are manipulative, abusive, irresponsible, who lie, cheat, are arrogant, disrespectful or inconsiderate? Forgiveness is a difficult topic because it calls us as human beings to a higher standard--the standard of grace and mercy. But when we don't forgive we run into a greater human dilemma: that of unforgiveness--where the pain of resentment and bitterness flows through our veins, quenching our spirits, breeding a cynicism about life, people, and God. Unforgiveness encases us in a miserable existence, changing our perception of the world and people from positive to negative, causing us to withdraw, priming us to see the world and people as hostile.

How would you define forgiveness? Here are some ideas:
- letting go of the blame.
- ceasing resentment.
- pardoning.

Forgiveness cancels a debt someone owes us and restores relationships and is the only solution in a world ridden with sin and evil to help us start over with people. Forgiveness gives us the opportunity to express love and grace to others.

What forgiveness is and isn't
Forgiveness is a choice, not a feeling. Forgiveness is not fair, it is not easy, and it is hard work. Forgiveness is when you decide to let someone else off the hook--when you elect to not get paid back or take revenge for a wrongdoing. When you withhold punishment.
Forgiveness is not turning a blind eye or ignoring what happened.
Forgiveness is not forgetting or denying what happened.
Forgiveness is not the same as reconciliation.
Forgiveness doesn't justify, approve or excuse the offense or offender.
Forgiveness doesn't always remove the consequences of the offense from the offender.
Forgiveness is a process that may include confrontation and exhortation.

Why we need Forgiveness
The state of anger creates the need to forgive. As soon as we become angry at someone or something we need the sweet relief of forgiveness, not only to grant it to others but to receive it for ourselves. We need forgiveness to bring our lives back into a state of harmony and peace.

What do religious leaders and writers have to say about the importance and process of forgiveness?
Phillip Yancey wrote: *"Forgiveness is another way of admitting, 'I'm human, I make mistakes, I want to be granted that privilege and so I grant you that privilege'. Forgiveness breaks the cycle. It does not settle all questions of blame and justice and fairness: to the contrary, often it evades those questions. But it does allow relationships to start over. In that way, said Solzhenitsyn, we differ from all animals. It is not our capacity to think that makes us different, but our capacity to repent, and to forgive. Only humans can perform that most unnatural act; and by doing so only they can develop relationships that transcend the relentless law of nature."*
Josh McDowell wrote: *"Forgiveness is the oil of relationships."*

No matter what religious background you come from or belief you hold – it may help you to know that forgiveness is an important aspect of spiritual life. Christians are told to "forgive as Christ has forgiven you." ı   In Judaism, if a person causes harm, but then sincerely and honestly apologizes to the wronged individual and tries to rectify the wrong, the wronged individual is religiously required to grant forgiveness. Islam teaches that God is "The All-Forgiving." Forgiveness often requires the repentance of those being forgiven. In Buddhism, forgiveness is seen as a practice to prevent harmful thoughts from causing havoc on one's mental well-being.

Forgiveness cancels a debt someone owes us and restores the relationship when restoration is possible. It is the only solution in a world ridden with sin and evil to help us start over with people and discover peace.

Lynette writes: Months after not receiving my Dad's inheritance from one of my sisters--I felt convicted to forgive her. I knew I had to let go of the anger. I wrote and told her how much I loved her and wanted to reconcile with her. It was not until thirteen years later that she and I finally reunited.

So how can you practically forgive someone who has hurt us? Here are some *Steps to Forgiveness*. Applying these steps to our lives can deliver us from bitterness and help us work toward forgiveness:

- Discover forgiveness: When you discover and experience forgiveness deeply in your own life, you have a foundation to offer forgiveness to those who have offended you. Many find their belief in God's forgiveness helps them forgive others also.
- Choose to forgive: You must make the decision to let go of bitterness and revenge and forgive others.
- Renew your mind: Challenge your mind with the truth and about how you need to be forgiven too. You may consider seeking your Higher Power for help in forgiving.
- Grant mercy: Empathize with those who have injured you. Recognize that forgiveness is the only way to be set free from the prison of resentment.
- Remember--forgiveness is a process: If you are stuck in unforgiveness, you can talk and pray with a confidante, a pastor, spiritual mentor, or a counselor to help you deal with the resentment and hurt you still feel. This will provide a context for release (of the painful feelings you are experiencing), support, and a better understanding of the person and situation.

When others (your partner) hurt or abuse us, when they disrespect or humiliate us, we can forgive them. So don't think that your anger should be stuffed down, negated, or turned into bitterness. Your anger is an emotion and force that can be useful. You can decide to forgive because that is a mechanism for resolving the hurts and the unfairness of life.

Guidelines for Reconciliation and Forgiving

1. Deal constructively with the root cause of anger toward the offending party.
   a. Ask: What am I angry about? What is my responsibility? What is the other person's responsibility?
   b. Forego retribution.
   c. Pour out your anger in prayer or to a confidante.

2. Plan a constructive confrontation.
   a. Apologize, if appropriate. *This is an important step in taking responsibility for any way you have offended your partner or someone else.*
   b. Use a soft, loving approach. Reflect on the fact that you need forgiveness as well.
   c. Be honest, yet tactful.
   d. Indicate the behavior change needed.

3. Choose to forgive.
   a. Release your partner from guilt and bondage.
   b. Let go of the demands you want to make on your partner.

4. Return good to your partner or the offending party.

5. Change your attitude toward your spouse or the offending party.

Here is a question many people and writers ask:
Does Forgiveness = No Consequences? One thing I've been thinking about is: am I willing to treat a person who has hurt me as well as I would treat those I consider my closest friends (assuming that it's appropriate to interact with the person who hurt me)? It seems to me that until I am, I'm falling short of God's standards. Does it mean that there should be no consequences for the sin?

Answer: In his book, Total Forgiveness Kendall addresses the issue of how we treat others after they have let us down or mistreated us. There are consequences which sometimes can't be and shouldn't be removed when we forgive. He talks about how a woman forgave the criminal who raped her but, decided to testify in court in order to stop him from inflicting another crime. In that case, judicial consequences were meted out along with forgiveness.

Here are some of my thoughts: You may decide that a friendship may change because that person cannot keep confidences. A change in relationship is not the same as forgiveness. You can let go of the blame and let go of any punishment and continuing to hold the wrong against a person--but, you may learn something about that person's character: that they can no longer be trusted with confidences or that they are not empathic and tend to be harsh when you divulge a weakness about yourself or that they are not responsible in keeping their commitments.

Therefore, you may forgive them, but, will no longer:
      … become vulnerable and share your mistakes
      … share your problems with them, or rely on them to do a project with you, etc.

Forgiveness does not mean that you will:
      ... trust all people on the same level or
      ... expect all people to live up to certain standards or
      ... relinquish the consequences for their wrongful behavior.

On the one hand, you can give someone another chance to start over but, on the other hand, there are times when you will need to set boundaries.

Forgiveness doesn't equal trust! Forgiveness doesn't mean there won't be consequences for the person. Forgiveness does not mean that boundaries will remain the same. Forgiveness will make you wiser. Forgiveness will challenge you at times to be vulnerable and to trust again. But, more importantly, forgiveness will set you free!

Questions for Thought

1. Define forgiveness. What makes forgiveness an important part of anger resolution? What are the consequences of hanging onto resentment? How does it affect your relationship?

_____

_____

_____

2. Think of times you could not forgive your partner. List all the excuses you have for not forgiving:
__ He/she has failed too many times.
__ He/she will do it again.
__ He/she will just take it for granted.
__ He/she hasn't asked for forgiveness.
__ The sin was too great.
__ The pain is too much.
__ I will not get over it.
__ He/she deserves to be punished.
__ He/she did it deliberately.
__ He/she is not really sorry.
__ other_____

Have you ever needed forgiveness? How does the quote by Phillip Yancey in this chapter affect your perspective on forgiveness and your need to forgive your partner?

3. What will happen if you decide to forgive your spouse/partner? What impact do the stories of forgiveness in the book have on you?

_____

_____

_____

"Forgiveness is a choice not a feeling. Forgiveness is not _fair,_ it is not easy, and it is hard work. Forgiveness is when you decide to _let someone else off the hook_ -- when you elect to _not get paid back or take revenge for a wrongdoing._ When you withhold punishment. Forgiveness _is not turning a blind eye or ignoring_ what happened. Forgiveness is not _forgetting or denying_ what happened. Forgiveness is not the same as _reconciliation._ Forgiveness doesn't _justify, approve or excuse_ the offense or offender. Forgiveness doesn't always _remove the consequences_ of the offense from the offender. Forgiveness is a process which may include confrontation and exhortation."

4. What is your opinion of this paragraph from the book? How does this change your perspective on forgiveness? Is it a possibility for you? How will forgiveness affect your relationship?

_____

_____

5. What is the hardest aspect of forgiveness for you? Which Steps to Forgiveness suggested in the book are you willing to take? What will the consequences be in the long-run?

_____

_____

_____

Foundational Insights: *Forgiveness sets you free from the prison of anger and resentment. Forgiveness ends the cycle of anger and blame moving you closer to reconciliation and new goals.*

6. How might you go about asking your partner for forgiveness for something which offended him/her? Why not try it now. Write it out and schedule a time to *ask* for forgiveness together.

_____

_____

_____

_____

_____

_____

7. Mary/Joe came home to find the house was a wreck after work and her/his spouse was home all day. She/he blew up and told him/her to clean up the house immediately or else. Her/his anger kept simmering over this event and she/he found it hard to act normally for over 2 weeks.

What's going on with Mary/Joe? Have you ever experienced this kind of anger?

_____

_____

How could she/he have handled the situation in a more appropriate manner?

_____

_____

_____

What if Question:
What if your partner says something negative about your character or generalizes by saying: "you always" or "you are just irresponsible"?

Your anger quotient is: 1-10 (1=low; 5= moderate; 10=high) _____

Your response is:

_____

_____

_____

What's good about your response (thoughts, behavior)?

_____

_____

Describe the consequences of your response:

_____

_____

How does this help you achieve your personal and relationship goals?

_____

_____

What do you need to change? How could forgiveness play a part in your respond?

_____

_____

The Prodigal Son Parable in "F"

Feeling footloose and frisky, a feather-brained fellow forced his fond father to fork over the family finances. He flew far to foreign fields and frittered his fortune feasting fabulously with faithless friends. Finally facing famine and fleeced by his fellows in folly, he found himself a feed-flinger in a filthy farmyard. Fairly famished he fain would have filled his frame with the foraged foods of the fodder fragments left by the filthy farmyard creatures. Fooey he said, My father's flunkies fare far fancier, the frazzled fugitive found feverishly, frankly facing facts.

Frustrated by failure and filled with foreboding he forthwith fled to his family. Falling at his father's feet, he floundered forlornly. Father, I have flunked and fruitlessly forfeited family favour. But the faithful father, forestalling further flinching frantically flagged the flunkies. Fetch forth the finest fatling and fix a feast. But the fugitive's fault-finding frater frowned on the fickle forgiveness of the former folderol. His fury flashed. But fussing was futile, for the far-sighted father figured, such filial fidelity is fine, but what forbids fervent festivity? The fugitive is found! "Unfurl the flags, with fanfares flaring! Let fun and frolic freely flow!" "Former failure is forgotten, folly is forsaken! And forgiveness forms the foundation for future fortitude."
Author unknown

Lesson Nine When to Take a Time-Out

> **Goals**: To explore how to apply a time-out for managing anger. To implement the time-out coping skill to help de-escalate anger.

*When angry count to ten before you speak.
If very angry, an hundred.*

Thomas Jefferson

Speak when you are angry and you will make the best speech you will ever regret.

Dr. Lawrence J. Peter

You may ask, "How do I know when to 'chill-out' or take a time-out? Usually I am well into the fight or argument before I know what is happening, and I can't stop the escalation. I feel like I have no control."

Step 1 is recognition of what makes you easily frustrated. What are your triggers? Against which people and in what situations does your anger escalate? Go to the provocation scenario to find out. Maybe you already know you are easily frustrated by:
- someone's tone of voice,
- the use of certain demeaning or critical words,
- glaring looks,
- disregarding or disrespectful behavior,
- someone not listening to you,
- feeling overwhelmed or helpless.

Step 2 is to be ready to say you have to take a break from such situations as soon as they occur. Anger rears its ugly head within one to three seconds. That does not give you much time to prepare, analyze, and control yourself.

Now that you have determined the times, situations, and people that trigger your anger, follow these guidelines:

Take a deep breath. (This will help your body calm down some and will help clear your mind.)

Pray. (Many people have found this helpful.)

Tell your partner: "I have decided to take a time-out to consider the issue(s) or problem(s)." It's good to have a prepared statement since anger can keep you from thinking clearly. (Write it out in your own words on a card and keep it in your pocket or purse if that helps.) "I will get back to you by _____." (Give a reasonable time-frame.) If this is a spouse, then get back to him/her within thirty minutes to twenty-four hours. A time-out is not an excuse to stonewall.

Don't apologize for taking a time-out. Nehemiah did this, and so can you!

Move to another part of the house, do something to cool down, listen to soothing music, do relaxation exercises, take the dog for a walk, or go to the coffee room at work.

When you are in your time-out period:
- Evaluate the scenario between you and your partner.
- Decide what the issue is and what your concerns are.
- Determine what you want or need. What request can you make?
- How can you reconcile if this is necessary or possible?
- Review Handling Anger Effectively, the assertiveness and conflict lessons and apply the recommended steps to your situation.
- Determine if you are struggling with any cognitive distortions and challenge your thinking with reality and the truth. Do you need to clarify something?

Questions for Thought

1. When have you applied the time-out to cool off in a relationship dispute? How did it help?

_____

_____

_____

2. What are the suggested steps involved in a Time-out from the book?

_____

_____

_____

3. List situations in your relationship when taking a time-out would help defuse anger/conflict:

_____

_____

_____

Foundational Insights: *Taking a time-out is essential to stop the escalation of (physiological) anger and conflict, calm down, identify the issue as well as your perspective and thoughts, and plan an intelligent approach for managing the conflict in your relationship.*

4. What impact does taking a time-out have on anger according to the Foundational Insights?

_____

_____

_____

The Good Book backs up the importance of taking a time-out: *"take note of this: Everyone should be quick to listen, slow to speak and slow to become angry, for man's anger does not bring about the righteous life that God desires."* [1]   Scriptures taken from the NIV translation.

Project: Review the time-out procedure. Write out the steps on a 3x5 card as a reminder:

Couple Discussion and Agreement for taking a time-out:

1. Discuss the pros and cons for taking a time-out. Agree to implement the following contract for 30 days.

2. Schedule a time to sign the couple's time-out contract or the following: *We will take a time-out whenever one of us recognizes that our emotions or the conflict/disagreement is getting out of control or could escalate. We will respect and comply with the request one of us makes to take a time-out. We will get back together to discuss the issue within 1-24 hours. We will apply the Handling Anger Effectively Steps to the discussion:*

Signed: _____ **Date:** _____

Signed: _____ **Date:** _____

What if Question:
What if you and your spouse or partner disagree about a vacation or disciplining the kids. Both of you begin to raise your voices.

Your anger quotient is: 1-10 (1=low; 5= moderate; 10=high) _____

Your response is:

_____
_____
_____

What's good about your response (thoughts, behavior)?

_____
_____

Describe the consequences of your response:

_____
_____

How does this help you achieve your personal and relationship goals?

_____
_____

What do you need to change? How could taking a time-out help the situation?

_____

78

Lesson Ten *Plan to Change Your Life by Changing Your Thinking.*

> **Goals**: *Determine how thinking can escalate angry feelings and behavior. Investigate how to change thinking that is distorted and unrealistic.*

Anger blows out the lamp of the mind.

Robert Green Ingersoll

It is important to recognize how much thinking impacts your feelings and can trigger your anger. Circle which type of thinking is true of you. If you cannot evaluate your type of thinking, ask a confidante or close friend or family member to give you feed-back.

Use the anger log sheet to evaluate examples of your thinking during angry scenarios. Compare and contrast it with this list to see where you might be struggling with cognitive distortions.

1. *All-or-nothing thinking*: You see things in black-and-white categories. If your performance is less than perfect, you consider yourself a total failure.
Give an example of how you may think this way. For example: "I (he/she) always come-up short." "I (he/she is) am just a failure." "I can't handle this."
Do you feel like a total failure at times or think your spouse is? Example: "I (he/she) can never make it work."

Is this a distortion of the truth?

Do others tell you that you are not seeing things clearly?

How often does this thinking pattern occur?
    daily   weekly   more than once a day   several times a day

With whom?   Where?

2. *Over-generalization*: You see one negative event as an unending pattern of defeat. Example: "We are always fighting" (even though this only happens once a week).

When do you think this way? What do you tell yourself?

How often does this thinking pattern occur?
    daily   weekly   more than once a day   several times a day

With whom?   Where?

3. *Mental filter*: One negative detail or event is all you can dwell on. Thus you think that most of life is pretty negative as well. Do you always see the cup as half-empty? Example: "We would have had a great time at the picnic, but my spouse disappointed me."
Do you dwell on the negative?

How often does this thinking pattern occur?
  daily   weekly   more than once a day   several times a day

With whom?   Where?

4. *Disqualifying the positive*: You believe that positive experiences "don't count" for some reason or other. So you maintain a negative belief about your life even though circumstances contradict it.
Describe when this type of thinking occurs: Example: "Even though I got a good evaluation, I know my boss hates me."

How often does this thinking pattern occur?
  daily   weekly   more than once a day   several times a day

With whom?   Where?

5. *Jumping to conclusions*: You automatically make a negative interpretation even though there are no definite facts that really support your conclusions.

How and when does this kind of thinking occur?

Example: "My spouse came home late; he/she must be having an affair."

How often does this thinking pattern occur?
  daily   weekly   more than once a day   several times a day

With whom?   Where?

a. *Mind-reading*: You indiscriminately conclude that someone is reacting negatively to you, and you don't bother to check it out. Example: "He/she went to lunch with another co-worker, so he/she must be mad at me."

When and how does this happen?   What do you tell yourself?

How often does this thinking pattern occur?
  daily   weekly   more than once a day   several times a day

With whom?   Where?

b. *The fortune-teller error*: You anticipate that things will turn out badly, and you feel convinced that your prediction is an already-established fact. Example: "I know I'm going to fail this class" (even though you are getting good grades).

When and how does this happen? What do you tell yourself?

How often does this thinking pattern occur?
    daily   weekly   more than once a day   several times a day

With whom?   Where?

6. *Magnification (catastrophizing) or minimization*: You exaggerate the importance of things (such as your goof-up or someone else's achievement), or you inappropriately shrink things until they appear tiny (your own desirable qualities or the other person's imperfections). This is also called the "binocular trick."
When and how does this happen? What do you tell yourself? Example: "He always wins" (even though you won the chess game last week) or "my body is too fat" (even though you have been told you are the right weight).

How often does this thinking pattern occur?
    daily   weekly   more than once a day   several times a day

With whom?   Where?

7. *Emotional reasoning*: You assume that your negative emotions necessarily reflect the way things really are: "I feel it; therefore it must be true."

When and how does this happen? What do you tell yourself?

If you fall into this category, you are depending on your feelings as the measure of truth.

How often does this thinking pattern occur?
    daily   weekly   more than once a day   several times a day

With whom?   Where?

8. *"Should" statements*: You try to motivate yourself with "shoulds" and "shouldn'ts", as if you have to be whipped and punished before you can be expected to do anything. "Musts" and "oughts" are also offenders. The emotional consequence is guilt. When you direct should statements toward others, you feel anger, frustration, and resentment. Example: "I should clean the house in two hours." This is also a sign of perfectionism.

When and how does this happen? What do you tell yourself?

How often does this thinking pattern occur?
    daily   weekly   more than once a day   several times a day

With whom?   Where?

9. *Labeling and mislabeling*: This is an extreme form of over-generalization. Instead of describing your error, you attach a negative label to yourself. Example: "I'm a loser." When someone else's behavior rubs you the wrong way, you attach a negative label to him or her: "She/he's a loser." Mislabeling involves describing an event with language that is highly colored and emotionally loaded.

When and how does this happen? What do you tell yourself?

How often does this thinking pattern occur?
    daily   weekly   more than once a day   several times a day

With whom?   Where?

10. *Personalization*: You see yourself as the cause of some negative external event that in fact you were not primarily responsible for.
When and how does this happen? Example: "If I had prayed more, my son wouldn't have had a car accident."

What do you tell yourself?

How often does this thinking pattern occur?
    daily   weekly   more than once a day   several times a day

With whom?   Where?

This material has been adapted from Resource for Cognitive Distortions (revised) by D. Burns.

Questions for Thought

1. What three cognitive distortions did you most identify with?

_____

_____

_____

2. How does this kind of thinking contribute to your anger? How does it affect your relationship?

_____

_____

_____

3. Do you tend to magnify situations or minimize? Do you use a mental filter or jump to conclusions? Do you tend to personalize or mind-read? Are you a fortune-teller or do you label your spouse or partner? Be specific as to how you do this with your spouse or partner?

_____

_____

_____

Foundational Insights: _Distorted and irrational thinking and expectations tend to escalate anger and conflict in relationships. When distorted thinking is challenged with reality and truth - effective anger management is possible and relationship satisfaction can be enhanced._

4. What effect does thinking have on your anger and relationship? Do you agree or disagree with the quote by Ingersoll?

_____

_____

An angry man is again angry with himself when he returns to reason. Publilius Syrus

5. Commit to change your thinking about your partner. Is it possible for you to believe the best instead of the worst about your partner? How can that happen?

_____

_____

_____

6. Write out exceptions or times when you found out your thinking was wrong. When did you mind-read, generalize, personalize or jump to conclusions about the actions or decisions of your spouse/partner and discover you were wrong?

_____

_____

_____

Did you challenge your thinking? Did other facts come to light which disproved your thinking?

_____

_____

_____

How could you have investigated the situation further with your partner to alleviate or change your thinking and thus, defuse anger and conflict?

_____

_____

_____

Assignment: Log your thoughts for the next week and challenge them with the truth and reality.

Ask yourself: What if I was to give my partner the 'benefit of the doubt' rather than judging him/her harshly? What would happen if I let go of the distorted thinking and believed the best about my spouse/partner when I am disappointed by him/her? How would this change our relationship? How would healthy thinking change my anger and any hostility I might harbor?

_____

_____

Try Humor Instead of Anger

Next time you are really livid about an inconvenience--like poor service--try making your point with humor instead of anger:
David went with his family to a fancy restaurant. Everyone ordered clam chowder. David noticed a gritty texture in the soup, scowled, and began to complain angrily. His nine-year-old son, Matt, also noted the grit but replied with a grin, "The clams are so fresh, you can still taste the sand in them!"

Log Your Thinking

An angry man is again angry with himself when he returns to reason.

Publilius Syrus

We encourage you to make a log of your thinking patterns as you use this course. Making a transition from unhealthy to healthy thinking is at times a difficult process but an important one.

Here is an example of faulty thinking:
"My friend showed up late for our dinner together. I concluded he/she really didn't want to be with me" (mind-reading).
What is the truth about this situation or person?

Describe the facts of the situation:
"Mary/Hank had a flat tire on the way to my house, which kept her/him from arriving on time. Therefore I should question the conclusion that she/he doesn't want to be with me. Maybe my low self-esteem is causing me to mind-read and jump to this negative conclusion."

We need to challenge such faulty thinking.

1. Give an example of a time when you used faulty thinking such as a time when your spouse/partner overlooked your needs or preferences.

_____

_____

_____

What is the truth about this situation or partner?

_____

_____

_____

Describe the facts of the situation:

_____

_____

_____

Ways to challenge my faulty thinking:

_____

_____

_____

2. Give another example of a time when you used faulty thinking.

_____
_____

What is the truth about this situation or person?

_____
_____
_____

Describe the facts of the situation:

_____
_____
_____

Ways to challenge my faulty thinking. How can you give him/her the benefit of the doubt?

_____
_____

3. What faulty thinking similarities do you see in the situations you have logged?

_____
_____
_____

4. What will it take for you to believe the facts and truth versus your faulty thinking when you are confronted with anger-provoking situations?

_____
_____
_____

PLAN TO CHANGE YOUR LIFE BY CHANGING YOUR THINKING
As you make such a plan and put it into action, the following questions and steps will be helpful:

1. What pattern of cognitive distortions do you see in your own Thinking? Which distortions occur most often?

_____
_____
_____

2. How can you challenge your thinking and bring about change?

_____
_____
_____

3. This quote provides a challenge and a goal to aspire to: *"Finally, whatever is true, whatever is honorable, whatever is just, whatever is pure, whatever is lovely, whatever is commendable, if there is any excellence, if there is anything worthy of praise, think about these things."* ₁

What effect will thinking the best of your partner versus the worst have on you? Is it possible?

_____
_____

4. How has your negative thinking pattern affected you emotionally, mentally, and spiritually-- maybe even physically?

_____
_____
_____

5. What can you do to begin changing your faulty thinking?

_____
_____
_____

Examples:
- Make a log of your faulty thinking patterns, and challenge them with the truth. ___
- Read inspirational resources daily, pray often. ___
- Talk with a confidante, counselor, pastor, and advisor. ___

6. How can you begin to think about whatever is true, noble, right, pure, lovely, admirable, and excellent in regards to your partner?

_____
_____
_____

How will thinking like this affect your life? How will it affect your relationship?

_____

_____

_____

Will you be less depressed? Less anxious? More optimistic? More hopeful?

7. Do you really want to get better? What would your life be like if you were more hopeful and optimistic?

_____

_____

_____

8. Have you tried such a plan before? Did it work? Why or why not?

_____

_____

_____

9. Which of these steps do you think will be the hardest? Why? What would help make it easier?

_____

_____

_____

10. How do you feel about the question, "Do you really want to get better?" Be honest. Why do you think this question is either fair or unfair? Helpful or irritating?

_____

_____

_____

11. What will it take for you to believe the facts and truth versus any faulty thinking when you are confronted with anger-provoking situations?

_____

_____

_____

12. Describe how thinking patterns and distortions can have anger-provoking effects?

_____

_____

_____

_____

Lesson Eleven — *How Emotional Intelligence Impacts Anger*

Goal: *To learn the importance of emotional intelligence - identifying how to empathize with others.*

The ability to understand and regulate emotions as well as understand the emotions of others and handle relationships constructively = emotional intelligence.

Emotional Intelligence Skills Help You Manage Anger

What does emotional intelligence have to do with managing anger? Maybe you are wondering, "Why should I learn about emotional intelligence? If I am keeping my anger in check, that should be enough."

Experts have discovered that people with a high degree of emotional intelligence (EI) are more motivated to manage their anger, get better results, and build healthy relationships. Wouldn't you like to experience the kind of life where anger no longer dominates you, but becomes one of the tools you use to achieve your goals and experience a more satisfying life?

Let's first take a look at the meaning of EI. Daniel Goleman writes, "Emotional intelligence is the ability to recognize your own feelings and those of others, motivate yourself, manage your emotions well and in your relationships."

Growing in anger management skills is helpful. But developing EI will improve your life in greater ways. How? Ari Novak, Ph.D., LMFT, a leader in Anger Management, attests to the importance of EI in managing anger. He states, "After treating clients with anger-related issues for over 7 years, I have come to realize that increasing skills in Emotional Intelligence (EI) is one of the most effective interventions a person can learn. EI skills improve performance in so many areas of life including leadership, intimate relationships, and simple day-to-day situations."

How Emotional Intelligence Works

When you develop Emotional Intelligence you become adept at the following:

1. *Self-awareness*. Self-awareness is having the ability to identify your own emotions, strengths, and weaknesses. This foundational step in EI provides the ability to monitor your feelings and determine what triggers your anger. People who lack self-awareness of feelings are more prone to becoming ensnared by them and being left at their mercy. By gaining the skills to watch carefully and oversee your feelings, particularly your anger, you will be able to identify what the issues are and make better decisions about responding to difficult situations. Find out how you are doing in the area of self-awareness by reviewing the "Anger Survey," "Power of Anger," and "Managing Stress" lessons.

2. *Self-management*. Self-management is the ability to effectively be in control of your motives and regulate your behavior. Self-management is built on self-awareness and provides the capacity for bouncing back from failure or disappointments. By gaining the ability to apply the cognitive and behavioral skills found in this book, you will become more proficient at controlling unhealthy anger and emotions and building effective skills to guide anger into assertiveness, problem-solving, forgiveness, time-outs, and healthy self-talk. Examine the lessons covering these skills and determine your level of progress in applying them.

3. *Self-motivation*. Self-motivation is monitoring and controlling one's emotions in order to achieve goals. This ability delays immediate and temporary gratification by stifling impulsiveness in order to accomplish projects and long-term objectives. When you see the bigger picture of reaping the consequences for your actions, you will be self-motivated to redirect your anger and emotions into healthy communication and behavioral skills. The concept of this book is that "you can have good anger." That idea has motivated many people to change. Go back to the "When Anger is Good" lesson. Ask yourself, "What consequences have I experienced from unhealthy anger? What are the pros for expressing my anger in healthy ways? How does this motivate me to change?"

4. *Social awareness*. Social awareness is gaining empathy for other people. Empathy is the capacity to understand what others are saying and feeling and why they feel and act as they do. Empathy is built on self-awareness, self-management, and self-motivation. When you are able to empathize, you will put yourself in other people's shoes, understand their feelings and viewpoints, and consider their needs. Review the "Managing Conflict" lesson. How have you applied the Sum-Up skill? What has been the result? Read the rest of this lesson to really learn the importance of and how to apply empathy.

5. *Relationship development*. Relationship development is the capacity to act in such a way that you are able to influence others without controlling them. This allows you to achieve personal and relational goals. When you employ assertiveness and empathy skills and negotiate issues while considering the best interests of all parties, you will develop healthy and compatible relationships with others. Your relationships will improve when you cultivate assertiveness, empathy, and conflict management skills (see the EI competencies list by Daniel Goleman and Hay Group). This book is geared to help you develop in the areas of self-awareness and self-management by understanding and managing anger, one of the most stressful and overwhelming emotions. You can learn anger's underlying causes and triggers and redirect it into healthy thinking and behavior.

Dr. Pfeiffer, President of NAMA and Growth Central writes, "The development of Emotional Intelligence initially means to recognize--actually feel--the sensations of frustration, annoyance, and anger in your body. Maybe you feel these in the form of tension in your chest, or you notice your face getting warm or red, maybe your hands are beginning to sweat. Once you are familiar and aware of these bodily sensations you are now ready to begin talking about your emotions as you actually experience them. The process of recognizing, experiencing and talking about your emotions puts you on the road to understanding and having compassion for yourself and then the ability to understand that others also have emotions too . . . you now have the capacity for empathy."

The Next Step: Learning to Empathize With Others
In order to really develop EI, we encourage you to focus on how to be a more empathic person as this is the key to social awareness and is critical to relationship compatibility.

First, take the empathy inventory found at the end of this lesson. Afterward come back and finish reading this lesson in order to identify the importance of developing empathy.

What is empathy?
Empathy is authentically listening to and understanding someone else's point of view. It's about seeing the situation from the other person's perspective. Empathy requires the ability to identify feelings and care about other people enough to consider their opinions and views, even when theirs differ from your own. Empathy will help decrease your frustration and anger-triggers because you will be focused on thinking about the other person's needs and not just your own.

Why is empathy important?
Empathy is the key to social awareness and is thus a key for defusing anger. By exploring someone else's viewpoint and feelings and putting yourself in the other person's shoes, you will be more likely to give the other person the benefit of the doubt and less likely to hold on to anger and resentment.

Gaining skills of listening to others and empathizing with them are essential for building relationships, defusing conflict and anger, and truly connecting with other people. It can build your relationships with those you interact with at your job such as customers, clients, and coworkers. It can also help bond, bridge, and mend personal relationships with spouses, family members, and friends.

Most of us spend 70% of the day communicating. With nearly three-quarters of our day spent communicating, you would think that listening would compose half of that communication. Yet only 45% of our time communicating with others is actually spent listening. Statistics show that spouses communicate only 10-20 minutes per day.

Listening and empathy skills are foundational to interpersonal communication, and yet surprisingly we are rarely taught these skills in the classroom or from our parents.

It is insulting to be ignored, interrupted, or neglected. We all want to be heard and understood. We want others to really care and understand our feelings and opinions. We want to know we matter. We want validation. And yet we have difficulty giving to others the very thing we want from them.

How is empathy expressed?
One of the best ways to validate and connect with others is to ask them questions about themselves and to really listen to their response. This "active listening" is briefly discussed in the lesson on Managing Conflict.

People love to talk about themselves. Write out some questions in advance of meeting with people that you can ask to help you find out more about who they are and what their lives are like. Then be prepared to genuinely listen. After they have shared, paraphrase what they have said. If you can paraphrase and summarize what someone has said to you, you will send the message that you were listening, you understand and care for that person. Listening and paraphrasing is one of the most effective and important ways to validate someone. Taking the time to understand someone and enter into their world is the first step to becoming an empathetic person. Empathy goes the extra mile. It listens with the heart. We all know what it means to really listen. Listening is more than hearing and processing words. Listening understands, affirms, and accepts the other person's meaning, experience, and feelings.

Here are some benefits from practicing good listening and empathy skills:
• You are able to care for and understand the other person. Often the conversation is directed toward emotional issues that are very important to others. As a result, people will enjoy talking to you and will open up more.
• Even if you misunderstand others, you allow them to correct your interpretations. As a consequence, you are able to grow and learn more about other people.
• You let the speaker know that you, the listener, accept the speaker. In return the other person will feel more comfortable telling his or her story and feelings to you. Since the speaker feels safe to talk about personal subjects with you, he or she will be more vulnerable by expressing his or her deeper emotions, exploring his or her emotions and problem-solving.
• It decreases any frustration or anger you may have.
• It can also promote forgiveness because we gain a greater understanding of the other person's experience.
• It can prevent or reduce negative assumptions about others because empathy helps us build understanding of the other person.
• It fosters meaningful, helpful, and close friendships.

You may be thinking that this is too much. You have enough problems and concerns of your own. You don't have the time or desire to concern yourself with other people and their needs. Or maybe you feel angry that no one has shown empathy to you and so you do not wish to show empathy to others. Perhaps you just want to "live your life" and not be bothered with learning and practicing empathy skills. But there's something in it for you, too. When you are empathetic with others, they are more likely to show empathy toward you. And as you practice empathy, you too will benefit from your actions as you will be on your way to liberating yourself from the negative patterns of bitterness and anger.

We believe that when you build your emotional intelligence skills, you will discover a greater ability to manage your anger, get better results, and experience healthy relationships. Challenge yourself to really grow by writing out and applying the following questions and assignments. Then you will discover the kind of life where anger no longer controls you but becomes one of the tools you use to achieve your goals and experience a more fulfilling life.

Foundational Insights:
Developing empathy is key to promoting deeper connection and understanding between people. Empathy provides awareness and sensitivity for the other person's point of view and experiences – thus defusing anger, cognitive distortions and conflict.

The following inventory is designed for personal use and for discussion. Check the characteristics and tendencies which best describe you thoughtfully and honestly. Do not score or read the instructions on the next page until you have completed the inventory. Permission is granted to provide one copy of the inventory and examples to the facilitator or group leader for feedback. Complete any examples required as instructed on the scoring page.

Empathy Inventory: © copyright 2012 by Lynette J. Hoy, NCC, LCPC
1. When I am talking with someone – I find it hard to listen: ___
2. When someone is speaking I generally am thinking about I want to say and miss what they have said: ___
3. When someone is speaking I usually ask clarifying questions so I can understand what they have said:___ (check if you go back later with clarifying questions)
4. When others are talking I try to paraphrase or summarize what they said: ___
5. When someone is talking about a problem I try to pick up on their feelings and say, "you seem stressed out by work or disappointed with your life": ___
6. Others have told me I am a good listener: ___
7. People come to me when they have problems for encouragement: ___
8. I try to see things from other people's point of view even when I disagree with them: :___
9. I try to impress on others the point I want to get across: ___
10. I turn conversations around or change the topic so I can say what I believe is really important: ___
11. I have difficulty identifying feelings and emotions in myself: ___
12. I have difficulty identifying feelings and emotions in others: ___
13. When someone seems troubled I generally ask them what is happening: ___ Provide a recent example here:
14. When someone doesn't share my opinion I either explain myself in greater detail or stop talking to the person:___
15. I can easily identify strengths and weaknesses in my life: ___
16. When someone shares a problem and their feelings – I explore what may be the cause with them: ___
17. When my goals are in contrast to others – I usually try to negotiate with those in disagreement: ___
18. Most people say that I am a caring, thoughtful person: ___
19. People complain that I am "self-centered": ___
20. Significant people in my life say that I am driven to achieve my goals: ___
21. Some people say that I'm a poor listener: ___
22. People say that I am able to manage my anger and emotions: ___
23. I don't find it necessary to pressure people into believing the way I do about something important to me: ___
24. I try to imagine what it's like to be in someone else's situation and what they might be experiencing: ___
25. When someone is angry or frustrated with me I have a hard time listening to their complaint or remarks: ___

Score the Empathy inventory:
A. Numbers 1, 2, 9, 10, 11, 12, 14, 19, 20, 21, 25 = 0 (zero).
B. Add 1 point each for numbers: 3, 4, 5, 6, 7, 8, 13, 15, 16, 17, 18, 22, 23, 24.
(provide recent examples for each one of the B category statements on another sheet)

Empathy rating: 0= Heartless; 2-4= Low; 5= Half-hearted; 6-10= Moderate; 11-13= High; 14= Bleeding Heart.

Questions for Thought

1. Write out 2-3 sentences that describe your understanding of emotional intelligence.
_____
_____

2. How can developing EI help you achieve your goals in your life and affect your relationship?
_____
_____

3. What is your opinion on the importance of empathy? How can empathy have an impact on your anger?
_____
_____

4. Circle your final score on the empathy inventory: Empathy rating: poor = 1-4; moderate = 5-10; high = 11-14.

5. From the Empathy Inventory provide recent examples of the "B" statements you checked on a separate sheet.
_____
_____
_____
_____

6. On a scale from 1-10 (1 being the lowest and 10 the highest) how motivated are you to develop empathy skills? Share your reasons for being motivated or unmotivated.
_____
_____
_____
_____

7. How will supportive, empathic communication positively change your relationship?
_____
_____

8. In order to determine your growth in self-awareness, self-management, and self-motivation complete the following questions:

   a. From the survey in lesson one which kind of people and situations generally trigger your frustration and anger? Give an example from your relationship?

   b. How do you normally try to calm yourself down? What phrases or thoughts help defuse your anger especially anger with your partner?

   c. What skills from the book do you regularly apply to stressful situations especially with your partner that trigger anger or frustration?

   Assertiveness:____
   Empathy:____
   Time-Out:____
   Problem-Solving:____
   Changing Self-Talk or Cognitive Distortions:____
   Forgiveness:____
   Stress Management and Relaxation:____
   Prayer:____

   d. What motivates you to develop EI?

   Rate your motivation level here:

   Low (1-3):____ Moderate (4-6):____ High (7-10):____

9. In order to determine your growth in social awareness, empathy, and constructive relationships, complete the following questions:

   a. Take the empathy inventory again in the appendix and rate yourself:____

   b. What skills are you applying to manage conflict and work through relationship misunderstandings?

   Paraphrasing, Sum-Up:____
   Active listening:____
   Time-out:____
   Assertiveness:____
   Problem-solving:____
   Forgiveness:____
   Other:____

c. What steps will you take this week to grow in empathy skills?

d. Which skills from the conflict lesson will help you develop a healthier relationship?

e. How will forgiveness play a part in enhancing your relationship?

What if Question:
What if you are ruminating about how your partner mistreated you or disrespected you?

Your anger quotient is: 1-10 (1=low; 5= moderate; 10=high) _____

Your response is:
_____
_____
_____

What's good about your response (thoughts, behavior)? Did you find yourself being empathic?
_____
_____

Describe the consequences of your response:
_____
_____

How does this help you achieve your personal and relationship goals?
_____
_____

What do you need to change? How could empathy "putting yourself in his/her shoes" help your response/attitude?
_____
_____

How's Your EQ? Review and complete the following. Be honest:

Self-Awareness: Capacity for understanding one's emotions, one's strengths, and one's weaknesses. When you don't recognize your feelings – it leaves you at their *mercy*. When you can monitor your feelings you can identify what the issues are and make better decisions about your life.

Describe your character strengths and weaknesses. Are you able to identify the areas in which you need to grow personally (honesty, responsibility, compassion, integrity or fear, laziness, anger, jealousy, criticalness, etc.?) Write some out here:

_____
_____
_____
_____
_____

Self-Management: Capacity for effectively managing one's motives and regulating one's behavior. This ability is built on self-awareness and provides the capacity for bouncing back from failure or disappointments. On a scale from one to ten (one being low ability to regulate behavior; 5 being moderate ability to regulate behavior and 10 being high ability to regulate behavior) what is your capacity for managing your motives and behavior? Write out an example (use another sheet):

_____
_____
_____

Self-Motivation: emotions are monitored and controlled in order to achieve goals. This skill delays gratification and stifles impulsiveness to accomplish projects and objectives.

In what ways are you able to keep your emotions in check and make responsible decisions in order to achieve goals? Example: "I can control my frustration and anger at work because I want to keep my job and pay the bills." Or "I won't buy a new TV or stereo until I have saved up enough money for it." I tell myself "it's worth the wait. I won't have to pay interest. This will make my life less stressful."

_____
_____
_____
_____

Social Awareness: Empathy is the capacity for understanding what others are saying and feeling and why they feel and act as they do. Empathy is built on self-awareness. Without self-awareness it's difficult to "put yourself in someone else's shoes." Take the Empathy inventory in the book or workbook and complete the questions.

Provide some examples of when you were able to show empathy to your partner?
Describe how well you listened? Were you able to paraphrase what your partner said to you?
Were you able to understand what your partner felt and identify what he/she might be feeling?

_____

_____

_____

_____

_____

_____

Relationship Management: Capacity for acting in such a way that one is able to get desired results from others and reach personal *and relational* goals. How are you able to influence your partner positively?

_____

_____

_____

_____

How have you helped your partner achieve his/her goals? How did you benefit and what were the results? When did you think about the best interests of your relationship and partner in achieving goals?

_____

_____

_____

_____

Lesson Twelve *Building Healthy & Successful Relationships*

Goal: *Identify ways to build healthy relationships through empathy skills and supportive communication and thus, defuse conflict and anger.*

Great relationships connect deeply resulting in closeness, collaboration and intimacy!

Validation and assertiveness are keys to helping you connect deeply with people. The *first key in connecting* is to be able to validate others through active listening and what is called "entering someone else's world". One of the best ways to communicate respect is to ask them questions about themselves and to really listen to what they say to you and pick up on their viewpoints through paraphrasing. You don't have to agree with their opinions, but you can show you value him or her as a person by *really* listening.

People love to talk about themselves--so be prepared to ask them some questions which will help you find out more about who they are and what their life is like. Then be prepared to really listen and paraphrase what they say. If you can paraphrase and summarize what someone has said to you, you will send the message that you understand and care for him/her. This is one of the most important ways you can validate another person.

When a husband says to his wife --
"Of course, what you have to say is important, it just isn't very interesting"-- his judgmental remark will cause her to feel invalidated, hurt and angry. *Asking questions and communicating support through paraphrasing skills expresses your value for someone else. Again,* You may not agree with what they are telling you, but, you can express understanding about what their life is like.... their problems, their struggles... This also helps you begin to empathize with people because you start putting yourself in their place and enter their world.

Validation is also expressed by communicating support and paraphrasing what someone is saying. When supportiveness and paraphrasing skills are combined with assertiveness the results are remarkably effective. With practice anyone can learn it!

SUPPORTIVENESS SKILLS:
These are abilities that help build trust and understanding between you and someone else and which communicates, "I'm on your side."

OPEN RESPONSES: This is the ability to communicate openness to help facilitate gaining further information, even if that information may be critical or emotional.
"....Say more about . . ."
"....I'm confused about . . ."
"....Spell that out further . . ."
"....Give me a specific example so I can understand more clearly."

Practice the following:
Open Responses:
-One person says, "You obviously don't care very much about old people!" You respond:

_____

_____

-Your spouse/partner says, "I always thought that you cared about fundamental community values. I can see now I was wrong." You respond:

_____

_____

(Use one of these open responses to explore further what the person next to you said about his/her motivation to attend the group or the goals he/she began considering because of the last session.)

UNDERSTANDING RESPONSES are best accomplished by paraphrasing: This is the ability to demonstrate to someone else, especially an antagonist, that you understand what he or she is trying to communicate. Paraphrasing is stating in your own words what the other person said.

First- Focus on the speaker (You . .)
Second- Be brief
Third- Summarize the Fact/Feeling

Here are some ways to help you paraphrase (repeated here from the assertiveness section):
"In other words..."
"Let me get this straight..."
"So you felt that..."
"What I hear you saying is..."
"If I understand you correctly..."
"Would you say that ...?"
"Do I understand you to mean...?"   "Do you mean...?"

Paraphrasing: Here are some Specific examples of Paraphrasing for empathic responses:
"You were really scared"
"You'd rather stay home because you are stressed out"
"You feel frustrated" or
"You felt it was very unfair for me to . . ."
"From your perspective I was not being helpful when I . . ."
"You were inspired to change when...."

If you can enter into your partner's world by reflecting back and paraphrasing what they have said--you will demonstrate empathy, concern and earn their respect. You will build bridges which draw you closer.

Let's try practicing these skills....

Ask your partner to describe a stressful event that recently occurred.
Paraphrase what he/she says.

_____

_____

Ask him/her: *How did you feel when I paraphrased what you said?*

Understanding Responses:

How would you paraphrase this complaint? Practice:
Your spouse says, "I just don't know how I'm going to make ends meet. We've had extra doctor bills this month. Then the car transmission went out & had to be replaced. Now you say we need a new washer. What am I going to do?"

You say:

_____

_____

Understanding responses....

Paraphrase the following:
Your partner says, "I'm trying my best to do a decent job. But how can I get everything done when there is so much to do?"

You say:

_____

_____

These skills will help you connect with your partner by validating what he/she says through paraphrasing skills. You don't have to agree with what he/she says. But you can show him/her *respect* and interested and validate what they said through these skills.

It is also important to be prepared to talk about yourself and to *develop the art of assertiveness as taught in previous lessons. Assertiveness is the second key to connecting with people.*

Foundational Insights:
Everyone wants to be understood and respected. Everyone wants to be heard. We can demonstrate our concern and respect for others through active listening and supportiveness skills. We can defuse conflict and anger with empathy.

Questions for Thought

1. What are some personal characteristics for building great relationships? How will supportive, empathic communication change your relationship? Write an example here:

_____

_____

2. How do you respond when someone really listens to you and displays empathy? Think of an example of when your partner or someone else expressed empathy towards you.

_____

_____

_____

3. What skills from this lesson are most helpful for you? How will these skills affect your relationship?

_____

_____

_____

4. Describe how applying the supportiveness skills can change anger and conflict escalation in your relationship?

_____

_____

_____

5. Apply some of these skills to a recent provoking scenario which escalated into conflict. How would the scenario have turned out if you had applied the supportive and/or paraphrasing skills? _Practice or rehearse a recent low conflict situation with your partner using these skills._

_____

_____

_____

6. Write out the understanding and paraphrasing responses on a 3x5 card to memorize.

_____

_____

_____

Lesson Thirteen   *Part I: Steps for HEALING the Wounds of Anger in Your Marriage by Lynette Hoy and Steve Yeschek*

Goal: *Apply listening with empathy; making requests with love and working towards healthy goals.*

Going deeper and making changes to really heal your marriage is a process. Hear with Empathy. Ask with Love. Imagine the Next Goal.

When lovers get angry

Do you ever wonder why there is so much anger in love? Why is it – we are able to hurt the one we love so much and he or she has so much power to hurt us? It may seem like a simple question – but, let's explore on a more personal level the dynamics of love and anger and how deeply marriages can be wounded..

People often write about the anger they experience in their marriages and intimate relationships. They describe anger as frustration, irritation, withdrawal, rage, stone-walling, harmful and explosive.

We know how to handle it when people who are just acquaintances mistreat us. We don't let it bother us. We shrug it off and say we don't care. Or we assert ourselves and stand up for our rights. But, when the one we love – the one we made vows to never leave or forsake years ago -- mistreats us - why can't we let it go? Why do we react with so much anger? And why do we feel emotionally wounded?

Andy recently shared how he and his wife, Sally, would get into arguments over little things – issues which really didn't matter much when they talked about it afterwards. What was really going on – I asked? He said that Sally didn't listen to him – that not listening to him was disrespectful. That feeling of disrespect and invalidation triggered his anger.

What about Sally? What was going on with her? What issues and triggers caused her anger? Was 'not listening' anger in disguise? Did she feel that her opinion didn't matter? Was she being treated with respect? Or did she feel controlled and insignificant?

Intimate, loving marriage relationships are complex. We hold different expectations for those we love. Our self-esteem rises and falls depending on the way our lover treats us. An intimate, loving relationship provides a safe place for us to be known, to be vulnerable, to be open more deeply than any other relationship and thus, to be wounded more deeply when our partner fails us.

When lovers treat us differently than we expect or desire – it triggers frustration, fear and anger. Often we mind-read what our lover is thinking or what his or her motives are for their behavior.

We want to be number one in the eyes of our lover. There is nothing like it... feeling needed, noticed, cared for and loved deeply for who we are and in spite of our weaknesses. But, when those needs and expectations are not met – we feel hurt and angry. We fear our spouse may leave us, humiliate us, disappoint us, reject us.

On the other hand, living well as a couple means living with an excellent skill set - a skill set for dealing with conflicts, for dialoguing and sharing information effectively, for relaxing and enjoying life, and also skills for emotional self-regulation. So, instead of getting agitated and angry, couples stay calm and are able to use their skill sets to deal with difficult issues.

WHAT ARE WAYS THAT COUPLES WOUND ONE ANOTHER THROUGH ANGER.

Recently, a couple I worked with fell apart from anger and isolation. Ashley withdrew her love from Trevor, husband of 2 years, because of his anger outbursts. The anger expressed by Trevor through yelling, criticism, and threats to divorce, led Ashley to withdraw from him physically and she retreated into relationships with people outside of the marriage.

Anger when not controlled can bring swift decompensation of any marriage. That is why scripture says, get rid of harmful anger. Regardless of the cause of the harmful anger, the result is always destructive.

There are so many hurtful ways that anger brings wounds into marriage. Through words, isolation, sabotage, intimidation, manipulation, withdrawal, coercive control, physical abuse, silence, and avoidance. Unhealthy anger brings pain without direction or resolve to move in the direction of problems solving, healing or love. Many husbands and wives live with the invisible pain of anger with one another.

It has been said, that "if you don't have anything nice to say about someone, don't say anything at all". Unfortunately, couples who abound with hurtful and angry words, bring long lasting harm to self-worth, mood, and the sense of emotional security. Words and attitudes of anger and contempt leave many couples bankrupt and devoid of security, safety, significance, and emptiness from a lack of love.

John Gottman categorizes destructive anger in marriage as 'the Four Horseman of the Apocalypse'.

1. Criticism:

Attacking your partner's personality or character, usually with the intent of making someone right and someone wrong. Generalizations: "you always…" "you never…" "you're the type of person who …" "why are you so forgetful…"

Many spouses experience a lifetime of anguish from words and attitudes of criticism.

The Bible says that "there is power of life and death in the tongue". Many partners are emotionally wounded and disabled from hurtful criticism. Scriptures exhort Christians to 'build one another up' and not tear each other down.

2. Contempt:

Attacking your partner's sense of self with the intention to insult or psychologically abuse him/her:

- Insults and name-calling: "wimp, fat, stupid, ugly, slob, lazy…"
- Hostile humor, sarcasm or mockery
- Body language & tone of voice: sneering, rolling your eyes, curling your upper lip

This behavior moves a spouse into feeling hated and unloved – causing a deeply troubled and unstable relationship.

3. Defensiveness:

This occurs when spouses see themselves as victims, warding off a perceived attack:

- Making excuses (e.g., external circumstances beyond your control forced you to act in a certain way) "It's not my fault…", "I didn't…"
- Cross-complaining: meeting your partner's complaint, or criticism with a complaint of your own, ignoring what your partner said.
- Disagreeing and then cross-complaining "That's not true, you're the one who …" "I did this because you did that…"
- Yes-butting: start off agreeing but end up disagreeing.
- Repeating yourself without paying attention to what the other person is saying.
- Whining "It's not fair."

Many couples allow anger to move them in the direction of defending and blaming and never coming to that place of humility, meekness, and love. To rebuild, each person must examine him/herself and take responsibility for what he/she can change.

4. Stonewalling:

Spouse often withdraw from the relationship as a way to avoid conflict. Partners may think they are trying to be "neutral" but stonewalling conveys disapproval, icy distance, separation, disconnection, and/or smugness:

- Stony silence
- Monosyllabic mutterings
- Changing the subject
- Removing yourself physically
- Silent Treatment

These behaviors are catastrophic to a healthy and happy marriage and must be prevented.

Living well as Christian couples means allowing the Holy Spirit to pour out His love through each partner when difficulties arise with the goal of serving, building up and wanting the best for that spouse and relationship.

We want to help you as a couple apply empirically supported and biblical strategies to your relationship to assist you to work through anger in healthy ways with the acronym HEALING.

HEALING -- STEPS FOR REAL CHANGE

Jack writes: "I have come to the realization that my anger is destroying my marriage. After one too many blow-ups recently, my wife got serious. It was a wake-up call to me and I'm trying to resolve my anger issues.

I was feeling pretty confident about not having any significant blow-ups because I want my wife to feel safe and I want my marriage to last. I realize that 15 years of letting my anger get the best of me -- it has taken its toll on her. Now I'm hoping for things to get "normal".

The past blow-ups were never physically abusive, but did get to the point where I said and did some things "for effect". e.g. once I began to pack my bags saying I've had it. Once I threw a hot dog that I was eating forcefully to the ground. Once I sped down the interstate way too fast. Etc. Unfortunately there are 15 years of these episodes and I can't afford another one. Please help me, Jack."

HEALING: *Hear with Empathy. Ask with Love. Imagine the Next Goal.*
The first step to change for Jack and other couples with anger outburst to is begin to hear –

HEAR with EMPATHY

HEAR: Hearing includes reflective listening. You not only want to hear your spouse – you need to hear yourself. Listen and mirror what your spouse shares. Watch his/her body language. Listen to your inner self-talk - changing any hot-self-talk or mind-reading assumptions. Jack says that he did some things "for effect". Those actions were hurtful and wounded his partner and relationship. Hearing and listening can prevent the escalation of defensiveness and anger.

How will hearing help your relationship get back on track? Learning to hear (how to listen) is the first critical step towards understanding your spouse's needs, wants and goals. It is the critical stepping stone for building intimacy and trust and thus, a healthy marriage relationship.

Scriptural insights: James 1:19-20
Learning to hear one's own messages – will identify the negative self-talk blocking listening and thus, relational growth.
This first step is "to hear" because this will block the negative self-talk "oh no, here she/he goes again'. Instead, by concentrating on what is being said – spouses block negative self-talk and behave-- as if "what he/she has to say is important". This affirms your spouse versus disregarding him/her. This initial intervention is critical to blocking the criticism and defensiveness which causes a downward spiral in marriage (4 horsemen syndrome).
What do you tell yourself when some conflict occurs which irritates you? Do you have "hot self-talk?" Do you say, "he/she thinks he/she can bully me" or "they deserve to be punished" or "no one deserves this kind of treatment" or "I'm outta here?" These phrases will escalate your anger and contribute to a hostile attitude. What you tell yourself will powerfully affect your choices, actions and any responses or consequences.

Write out the self-talk which hinders listening to and really hearing your spouse:
_____
_____
_____

What about telling yourself something different such as: "he/she is having a bad day" or "maybe he/she didn't know how this would affect me" or "I'm not going to think about this now – I'll take a walk or a break and pray. I'll concentrate on what the real issue is."
Write out how you can change your self-talk. What phrases will you concentrate on?
_____
_____
_____

Write out what you have said to yourself in the past when you've been irritated or angry:

_____
_____
_____

Write out what you could say to yourself instead:

_____
_____
_____

Now, write out how you can respond in a healthy way:

_____
_____
_____

What normally happens to you when anger arises? You put earplugs in your ears and don't really listen because you become immediately defensive.
You think and maybe say: "there you go again – always complaining!"
Instead of thinking or saying: "what I hear you saying is that you are stressed out when I don't pick up my clothes".

Examples of active hearing and listening:
"I see that you are upset."   "You seem very distressed (or disappointed)."
"I hear what you are saying..."   "I can see how this would be very distressing."
"It can be stressful to go through this."   "I hear you. Most people would be upset."
    you don't need to agree or make a conclusion.

Repeat/Reflect/Summarize what he/she says:

"In other words . . ."   "Let me get this straight . . ."
"So you felt that . . ."   "What I hear you saying is . . ."
"If I understand you correctly . . ."   "Would you say that . . . ?"
"Do I understand you to mean . . . ?"   "You feel frustrated because ..."

Questions to motivate and explore:
Write out the triggering situations for your anger? Write out your self-talk:

_____
_____
_____

What have you done in the past that has worked?

_____
_____
_____

When have you really listened to your spouse? Describe what you did and how it helped the dialogue?

_____
_____
_____

Which 'thinking ahead reminders' from the book could help prevent escalation of anger with your spouse?

_____
_____
_____

Try out reflective listening now:

Write it out a situation.

_____
_____
_____

Write out what you say and what your spouse says.

_____
_____
_____

Complete the following:
If I listen more intently to my spouse – I will…….(mirror what he/she says; look directly into his/her eyes; I will be open to learning, etc.)

_____
_____
_____

Ask: What do you hear from within about your self-talk? What do you need to hear yourself say? Ex: instead of "she/he always is annoying me"… say, "he/she is talking to me and I can listen"

_____
_____
_____

Ask your spouse for an example of when you really listened to him/her:

_____
_____
_____

EMPATHY is the ability to put yourself in your spouse's place and understand your spouse's (deeper) feelings and viewpoints. Empathy is the ability to identify and understand another's situation, feelings and motives. It's your capacity to recognize and have *compassion* for the concerns of your spouse not just focus on your needs.

"Fred had to learn to empathize with Sue. He had to learn ways to really understand the impact of his emotional, and verbal abuse with Sue. To learn empathy, Fred prayed that no matter what Sue did, he would allow God to show him his sin. (Pride, fear of what people thought, anger). He prayed that God would give him Godly sorrow so that he saw he was sinning against God and his wife.

Fred used the principles of Jesus's Words to model his prayer to God to give him empathy and compassion toward the wound he had caused. (Poor in Spirit, mourning his sin, being meek in obeying God to turn from his anger, hungering and thirsting that he would do what was right, and being merciful).

Fred's prayer to God was – "no matter what caused me to get angry, show me my sin". God was faithful and led him to many points of repentance and healing."

Empathy is critical to develop emotional awareness to connect and love more deeply. Empathy builds emotional connection and oneness. "Empathy is the oil that keeps relationships running smoothly. Empathy makes the effort to stop and think for a moment about the other spouse's perspective in order to begin to understand where they are coming from. And then we need the emotional capacity to care for that person's concern " Daniel Goleman

Couples rarely empathize with each other during a conflict. Often, they don't hear each other and misinterpret each other's motives and words.

When your spouse says, "I just can't take all the responsibilities around here anymore!" What if instead of responding: "you just don't really care about my needs!" … "I can't take your complaining anymore!" You said, "I am concerned because you sound so stressed out"… "is there something I can do to help out?"

Write out a situation/issue your spouse is going through:

_____
_____
_____

What are his/her feelings about this issue? How can you see and even feel his/her emotions and viewpoint?

_____
_____
_____

If you were in your spouse's shoes – how would you feel/respond?

_____
_____
_____

What scriptures would apply? (carry each other's burdens, etc.).

_____

_____

_____

How does empathy help you show your spouse more compassion?

_____

_____

_____

Write out prayer asking God to help you be more empathic with your spouse:

_____

_____

_____

ASK with LOVE
ASK:
Asking is a critical step in good communication and for managing conflict with your spouse. Asking includes: assertiveness, clarification, exploring, encouraging, requesting, confessing. Communicating and discussing issues/situations more thoroughly clears up misunderstandings and assumptions. These skills lessen the likelihood of serious conflict. Effective dialogue is almost always collaborative.

Good communication includes listening (really hearing), empathizing and asking -- it is foundational to effective collaboration and conflict resolution. Applying empirically-supported strategies to relationships -- reduces anger and conflict and the wounds that result.

Transformational scripture: Prov. 20:5 "The purposes of a person's heart are deep waters, but one who has insight draws them out."

Bob writes, "Recently I was having an emotionally charged discussion with my spouse. This of course means that we both felt strongly about the topic and had opposing viewpoints. I was able to look ahead and see how the conversation was going to unfold, so I stopped talking. I started asking questions to understand her viewpoint. This is much easier to do when I remind myself that she is not trying to hurt me, she really loves me, and she wants the best for both of us. It's amazing what some corrected thinking can accomplish."
Notice how this husband applies a time-out, uses clarifying questions, corrects his thinking and uses empathy to try to understand her view point. These steps and skills keep anger and conflict from escalating. This is a healthy example of how to work through anger.

Practice Questions for couples:

Your spouse says:

_____

_____

_____

You respond: Tell me more about your feelings/view?
    So what you are trying to say is…. Did I get that right?
    What else would you like to say about this?
    What would help you feel more hopeful/encouraged about this issue?
    What can I do specifically to encourage you?
    How could we go about coming to a resolution about this issue?
    I apologize for causing you to feel hurt and/or for hindering the process by… (not listening, getting frustrated too easily, being curt, etc.). What more could I do to help?

Write out your response here:

_____

_____

_____

Bringing up a request or issue:

May I share what I have been feeling/thinking recently?

Not: I feel it's inconsiderate of you not to call me when you are going to be late"

Instead: When you are late and don't call – I feel worried.." "I would like to make a request…"

_____

_____

_____

What scriptures apply?

_____

_____

_____

How can you confess and apologize for something you did/said that hurt your spouse?

_____

_____

_____

How could you communicate differently to help improve understanding between you? Ex: use 'I' statements vs. 'You' statements (tends to sound blaming). Bring up issues when you and your partner are not stressed out or can plan a set time to discuss business/responsibilities.

_____

_____

What more needs to happen to bring about communication change?

_____

_____

_____

What could you do to bring about the communication changes that will improve your relationship? Ex: show more humility. Keep calm. Slow down my responses and 'think the best'.

_____

_____

_____

Write out some ways you can speak the truth in love? Ex: "I know you have a lot on your plate. But, I am wondering if I can make a request?" "What you said just now hurt me. I know you didn't mean to do that."

_____

_____

_____

What else could you do?

_____

_____

_____

LOVE: unconditionally. Love covers a multitude of sins. Accept where you are and who you both are. Forgive the past. Grant another chance – giving the benefit of the doubt (positive sentiment override).

For Fred to understand Loving his wife, he had to heal the wounds from his family of origin where his father was abusive to him…He had to feel the pain of the negative things his Dad had said, and change the thoughts, forgive his Dad, and begin to love himself through God's love., then he could love his wife.

Without forgiveness there is no love. Forgiveness is the key to the love of God and the Spirit of God moving in and through a marital relationship. True forgiveness starts with God. Without the forgiveness of God from God through the work of Jesus Christ and the death on the cross, there is no eternal life and no relationship with God. And, there is no restored relationship in a marriage without forgiveness for things done in the relationship.

I met with a couple married for 20 years. Bill is a recovering alcoholic that had recently relapsed and was resurrecting hurtful anger toward his wife, Julie, in an effort to take the focus off his drinking. Bill blamed Julie for 'disrupting his high' by 'nitpicking'. Rather than realizing that he had a problem with anger due to poor impulse control from his relapse into alcohol he remained in denial. Everyone but Bill knew he had a problem. It wasn't until in an intervention that he heard person after person say, "It's you Bill. You are the one who has a problem with alcohol and anger." Julie was ready to divorce unless Bill regained his sobriety and ceased from being so angry.

As Bill agreed to recommit to working the 12 steps and gain a sponsor, he and his wife needed to forgive one another and begin to love one another as the initial steps to healing. With humility and a desire to do the right thing, Bill and Julie were now on a road of restoration. I asked each of them to come up with a list of resentments to surrender to Christ and to vow to move forward in their relationship. When apologies were made and commitments to change were made, reconciliation moved deeper toward tender-hearted loving care.

Forgiveness requires humility, meekness, and strong desire to do the right thing and a commitment to let go of resentments and bitterness. Couples need to forgive in the power of the Holy Spirit and faith the God gives power to give victory over unforgiveness.

There also, in practicing forgiveness, has to be a commitment from couples to not bring up the past as a way of punishing one another. There must be a commitment to move forward in love.

Will you commit right now to move forward in love? What steps can you take to commit?

_____

_____

_____

Insights to Move Forward in Love
The Bible says that love is the greatest of virtues in First Corinthians 13.
'Love in an understanding way'. That means to love in a way that is perceived as love by the partner.
God's Word says, 'love is patient and kind.' These two traits go together. Patience is good, but to love, there must also be kind words, gestures, service, gifts and tender touch added. Couples need to be patient in withholding hurtful words of criticism, put downs, and negativity, but they must also be intentional with objective kindness.

'Love does not envy or boast'. Sometimes, couples envy the other's job, their talent or their relationships. Love chooses to stop that. Sometimes couples will boast about how much money they are bringing in or how much they do to keep the household going only to produce anger.
'It is not arrogant or rude'. We are, as spouses, to be tenderhearted and sensitive to cherishing our spouses. At times couples become more careless with words with their spouses than they are with co-workers or friends. That should not be so.

'It does not insist on its own way;' Love considers the others need as more important than their own. How easy it is for one or both in the marriage to get selfish and demanding. The Bible says to husbands in Ephesians 5:25, "Husbands, love your wives, as Christ loved the church and gave himself up for her, that he might sanctify her, having cleansed her by the washing of water with the word,…" It goes on to say, Husbands should love their wives as their own bodies. He who loves his wife loves himself." That clearly is going in the opposite direction of 'insisting on your own way'. Simple consideration of the others needs before your own. That seems strange in a selfish culture but true unconditional love is counter-cultural.

Love is not provoked. To not be provoked a person has to be prepared to 'not take things personally', to be aware of internal cues that lead to reactivity. Love is not provoked because one has the lens of acceptance of self and spouse. Self-talk based on total acceptance has to take the lead. Patience and grace are needed to deescalate the provocation and internal cues.

'Love does not take into account a wrong suffered, does not rejoice in unrighteousness, but rejoices with the truth'; To make that happen, couples need to practice ongoing forgiveness, learn to 'cover a multitude of sins' and to abide in the truth of unconditional love. That has to be the confession. "The other is more important than what they did wrong." "I will treat my spouse according to who they are in Christ, as a forgiven, loved, and accepted individual.' Forgive in the way you have been forgiven by God. That is the truth to rejoice in and act upon.

Love bears all things, believes all things, hopes all things, endures all things. Couples need to pray for this love that perseveres in forgiveness, patience, kindness. Couples need to hope through the Holy Spirit that God is working as they pray for one another. We have faith and hope that God is working 'all things together for good for those who love God and are called according to His purpose. That is how we endure, and we trust and look to God's love.

Love never fails. That is the greatest thing, the love of God operating in a marriage.
Scott Chapman talks about being proactive and conscious of loving through words, gifts, service and loving touch. As we think about those 'languages of love' we are reminded that the right word at the right time can not only pacify anger but heal a hurt. Gifts can also pacify anger and give a direction of love and affection. Service can also redirect a person away from anger and toward acceptance. And, loving touch at the right time confirms comfort and love put appeases anger.

Active listening and empathy are vital to turning fear and anger toward love. I met with Jane and Todd. Jane had experienced many painful memories of childhood abuse. Now, as a 50 year old woman, she had many triggers that caused her to be anxious when her husband was defensive or angry. Todd learned to listen to Jane's anxiety. He learned to use words of understanding, empathy and compassion. As Jane talked about the painful memories with her husband, Todd learned to express physical comfort and loving words and prayer. Jane experienced healing from the abuse and security as she shared with her husband about current and past issues of fear and fear of punishment.

Positive Sentiment Override – PSO
It has been found that married couples with high satisfaction in their relationships have a high PSO. The positive comments and behaviors outweigh negative ones about 20:1. It's almost as if there is a positive filter that alters how couples remember past events and view new issues.
For example, Steve and Deb have been connecting positively with each other over the past week – a dinner date, lots of sharing, they made love yesterday and are planning a weekend getaway. Steve sees milk spilt on the kitchen counter and asks Deb to wipe it up when she has a minute because he is busy on the computer. She replies that it's no problem and would he like a cup of coffee.

Very different from the scenario where Steve and Deb have been distant, hardly connecting with each other over the past weeks. PSO makes a huge difference in relationships for the simple reason that relationships and marriages that thrive, also have a strong PSO.

Obviously relationships don't automatically have a Positive Sentiment Override. The warmth, trust, affection, caring and a host of positive emotions which we call PSO have to be nurtured, developed and maintained over time.

I asked Fred and Sue to express forgiveness and love to one another. I asked them what words would most likely help them to feel forgiven. What embrace would help? What comfort words would help?

Questions:
What would it be like if you could forgive each other?

_____
_____
_____

How can forgiveness happen? Where can you start?

_____
_____
_____

When have you forgiven your spouse? What was the result?

_____
_____
_____

Have you considered giving your spouse the benefit of the doubt?

_____
_____
_____

What loving behavior can you share this week?

_____
_____
_____

Write out a prayer asking God how you can serve your spouse.

_____
_____
_____

Assignment:

Complete the HEAL practice activities at the end of the book.

116

Lesson Fourteen   *Part II: Steps for HEALING the Wounds of Anger in Your Marriage by Lynette Hoy and Steve Yeschek*

Goal: *Building your relationship by really listening with empathy; making requests with love and imagining the next goal.*

Going deeper and making changes to really heal your marriage takes time and is a process. Commit to: Hear with Empathy. Ask with Love. Imagine the Next Goal.

IMAGINE the NEXT GOAL

IMAGINE: with hope that your relationship can improve. Picture what that will look like. What will that mean for you regarding change? Remind yourself to think the best of your spouse. Consider how Jesus Christ can change you and your spouse and your marriage can become a reflection of His love to the world. Couples consider -- What would it be like if things were different/better? How would our relationship improve? Practically, spiritually and emotionally?

Bob: "Recently I was having an emotionally charged discussion with my spouse. This of course means that we both felt strongly about the topic and had opposing viewpoints. I was able to look ahead and see how the conversation was going to unfold, so I stopped talking. I started asking questions to understand her viewpoint. This is much easier to do when I remind myself that she is not trying to hurt me, she really loves me, and she wants the best for both of us. It's amazing what some corrected thinking can accomplish."Here Bob 'thinks the best' of his spouse, i.e., "I remind myself that she is not trying to hurt me, she really loves me and she wants the best of both of us."

Imagine that your relationship is more satisfying? Write out what that would look like?

_____

_____

_____

What would you be like? How would your thinking and behavior change?

_____

_____

_____

What else needs to happen for you to help your marriage be more satisfying?

_____

_____

_____

NEXT: consider -- what's next? What's possible? What step could I take to move us forward? To maintain progress over negative patterns of anger and healing wounds of anger, couples need to:

1. Continue praying for one another on a daily basis. Continue confessing faults to one another (fear, shame, anger, offenses, sins, struggles) and pray for one another for healing. Couples that pray together experience the power of the Holy Spirit that provides 'comfort, leading in truth, direction, and guidance'. Couples that pray together will increase compassion for one another and many troubles of the flesh and spirit are resolved.

2. Read the Word of God together. Couples that read and study scriptures together will not only increase their faith in God but also increase their sense of safety, significance, and security in the marriage relationship. Couples who have never done this before need to start out slow. Maybe reading a chapter a day in the New Testament and praying for application and wisdom regarding the relevance of the scripture to their relationship.

3. Daily Practice the love language. 'Love covers a multitude of sins' and calms many quarrels. Be proactive and intentional in using words of acceptance, approval, appreciation, admiration, and kindness. Loving words will break the power of hurtful anger. 'Don't forget to communicate'.

Vulnerability and Honesty.

Couples need to take the next step of increasing vulnerability and honesty about everything to increase emotional and spiritual intimacy. This, of course, can only happen when there is a desire to commit to the relationship.

Be intentional with loving physical touch. Couples need to sit together, to hug, to hold hands, to caress. It not only calms anger but brings warm feelings of love and security.

Daily serve one another in ways that the other feels loved. Serve by doing household duties, running errands for the other, helping with the children, etc. Serve as the Bible says, 'Husbands, serve your wives as Christ served the church and gave Himself for her.'

Give gifts on a regular basis. It doesn't need to be expensive. It does need to be special and thoughtful but doesn't necessarily need to cost money.

Spend quality time together. We need quality and quantity of time together as spouses. Date, take vacations together and have plenty of conversations about everything.

Love builds a reservoir of emotional security that is there to heal anger.

Explore positive (empirically-supported) strategies/behaviors that can be applied, i.e., time-out, respectful assertiveness, empathy, problem-solving approaches, change thinking, forgiveness, PSO, etc.

Write out which skills you have applied? What was the result?

_____

_____

_____

What would you be willing to do to help make the change to move your relationship forward?

_____

_____

GOAL: Write out your own Relational Change Plan.

Relational Change Plan:
What would your relationship look like and be like if you could manage anger and work through the hurt/anger/resentment?
Describe an angry scenario you have had with your spouse. What happened?

_____
_____

How did you react and respond to the conflict with your spouse? (blaming, minimizing, stonewalling, defensive, verbal outrage, empathy, listening, withdrawal, etc.)

_____
_____

How has this kind of response affected your relationship? Describe:

_____
_____

What is your Goal? Describe how you would like to handle anger in healthy ways:

_____
_____
_____

What types of Interventions will help you reach your goal?
Replay the scenario above in your head. How could you have reacted more positively or openly?

_____
_____
_____

What would it look like if you were to respond by demonstrating responsibility, love, empathy?
Write out how you could express responsibility, love, empathy:

_____
_____
_____

How will the new responses improve your relationship? How will your new responses affect future conflict and your anger quotient?

_____
_____
_____
_____

HEALING Change Steps:
Circle and complete the HEALING steps listed below you are willing to work on.

Hear with Empathy:
How you will commit to listen more intently to your spouse? Describe:

_____
_____
_____

How will listening benefit your relationship?

_____
_____
_____

What can you do to be more empathic?

_____
_____
_____

How will empathy change your relationship?

_____
_____
_____

Ask with Love:
Which of the steps can you begin applying in your marriage? Explore? Clarify? Confess? Share?

_____
_____
_____

How will applying the Ask skills change your relationship?

_____
_____
_____

What are some good questions you can ask your spouse to move forward? Write these out here:

_____
_____
_____

How can you make amends for something you have done to hurt your spouse? Write it out here:

_____
_____
_____

How can you offer forgiveness which is integral to real love?

How can you better serve your spouse? What will serving – even sacrifice -- look like?

(I would start doing my share of the household chores; decrease spending so much money for lunch or recreational activities; get involved in helping with the kids)

_____

_____

_____

What step can you take to forgive your spouse? How can God help you?

_____

_____

_____

Write out what you will you say to your spouse about forgiveness?

_____

_____

_____

As a couple – discuss "How can we apply the forgiveness process from the book?

_____

_____

_____

How will serving and forgiving affect your relationship?

_____

_____

_____

Imagine the Next Goal:

What would it be like if things were different/better? Ex: We would apply anger management skills or we would think the best of each other or we would forgive each other. Write out your own examples here:

_____

_____

_____

How would our relationship improve? Practically, spiritually and emotionally?

_____

_____

_____

How will you know that your relationship is better?

_____
_____
_____

What can you personally do to improve your relationship? What else?

_____
_____
_____

Next move (positive act):
What positive (empirically-supported) strategies/behaviors can you apply now to improve your relationship? (time-out, respectful assertiveness, empathy, problem-solving approaches, change thinking, forgiveness, etc.

_____
_____
_____

How will your relationship improve as you increase positive behaviors?

_____
_____
_____

What Goal will move you and your spouse towards real change?
Couple goal:
(bring up issues in a calm manner; take a time-out when I feel angry; pray daily for my marriage; practice empathy; listen intently; demonstrate love, etc.)
I will
_____
I will
_____
I plan to
_____
This week I will
_____

We have agreed to
_____
(a time-out when disagreements occur; pray; talk respectfully; etc.)

ANGER MANAGEMENT PROGRESS REPORT:
Week ___:
1. Anger Survey results (circle one): Category 1   Category 11   Category 111
2. Identify triggers in your relationship:

3. Identify present coping skill use in your relationship:

Please measure your use of anger coping skills in your relationship from 1-10: _____
(1=poor use of skills; 5=intermittent use of skills; 10=consistent use of skills)

4. How is your anger presently affecting:

Work:	greatly	moderately	little	none
Marriage:	greatly	moderately	little	none
Family:	greatly	moderately	little	none
Friends:	greatly	moderately	little	none
School:	greatly	moderately	little	none
Legal:	greatly	moderately	little	none
Personal	greatly	moderately	little	none
Goals:	greatly	moderately	little	none
Other:	greatly	moderately	little	none

(describe other :_____)

5. Describe one angry or frustrated episode/situation in your relationship from this week. What happened?

What triggered your anger?

What were your thoughts?

How did you respond towards your partner?

What skill did you try to use? Was it effective?

Underline the following coping skills from the book and workbook which you could implement in the future? (time-out, assertiveness, problem-solving, let it go, change thinking, forgive, pray, conflict management skills, avoid triggers, etc.) How have you improved? How was your relationship affected by your use of any of these skills?

*Course participants are granted permission to duplicate this page for personal use only.

Lesson Fifteen   *Stopping the Blame-Game*

> **Goal:** *Acknowledge and take responsibility for harmful anger. Identify the consequences of your actions.*

When you take responsibility for your behavior and anger – you can begin to control it.

It's not easy to own-up to our faults or lack of responsibility. When you are late to work – you tell the boss the traffic was horrible or your spouse didn't put the alarm on.

When you fail to pay the bills on time – you yell at your spouse for not reminding you or say that you thought it was his/her turn to pay them.

Blaming defined is: making it look like someone else is responsible for your actions and misbehavior.

Why is it so difficult to own-up? Why do people keep blaming and shirking responsibility or accepting consequences for their behavior? Maybe it has to do with pride? Maybe you learned that it worked to keep blaming and made *you* look good and *someone else* look bad. Maybe it's hard to be humble. Maybe it has to do with needing to be in control again.

Whatever the reason or excuse you make for blaming and not accepting responsibility – *it is not in your best interest or in the interest of building your relationship* to continue on this path.

How does blaming and not taking responsibility contribute to anger? It creates within you a defensive reaction. When situations occur and you are confronted with the truth of your behavior or you suffer consequences – like a slimmer paycheck because you haven't put in enough hours at work – you tend to blame it on someone else. Your spouse. Your boss. A co-worker or friend. You displace your anger onto someone else because you don't want to own-up. You don't want to feel bad about yourself or look bad in front of others. Blaming keeps you from being honest and taking the responsibility. You may feel better temporarily – but, in your heart you know the truth. You know you need to own-up.

The first step is to admit you have been living this way. Write out the situations when you have blamed someone or something else for your irresponsible behavior.

Make a Plan to Change:

Describe the situation:

_____
_____
_____

How did you react to the consequences? Did you blame someone else or minimize your behavior?

_____

_____

_____

How has this kind of behavior (blaming/irresponsibility) affected your work or relationships?

_____

_____

How did it affect your anger quotient? Retake the anger survey in the book and evaluate your response.

_____

_____

_____

Replay the scenario in your head. Who was really to blame? Maybe you were only partially at fault…

_____

_____

_____

How could you have responded by demonstrating responsibility?

_____

_____

_____

What would have happened if you took responsibility? How would this have affected the conflict, your anger quotient and your relationship(s)?

_____

_____

_____

Foundational Insights:
Taking responsibility is not easy. Taking responsibility means that you have to identify your on-going strengths and weaknesses. It means you have to be willing to become vulnerable. It may mean that you incur a negative consequence at work, in the community or at home.

Positive, long-lasting results generally come from taking responsibility vs. shifting the blame to someone else. People will trust you and your word. People will accept apologies from you. People may be more apt to own-up to mishaps and more apt to apologize to you. You will no longer have to hide behind a banner of blaming.

Lesson Sixteen *Enjoying the Benefits of Good Anger*

> **Goal:** *Assess the consequences of harmful anger and increase commitment to change.*

Consequences can be motivators for positive change.

One of the major reasons you are taking this course is due to consequences you have incurred because of acting out your anger. Maybe you got in trouble with the law. Maybe you were involved in a "road rage" incident. Maybe your behavior became threatening or violent or you injured your spouse, someone else or someone's property. Maybe your marriage is on the brink of divorce due to your anger. Maybe drinking triggered an angry outburst. In any case, you are suffering the consequences of expressing your anger in a harmful way.

Harmful anger has disrupted your life. It may have caused a rift between you and your spouse or another significant person in your life. Your anger may have caused you to lose your job, money and reputation. In the long-run, suffering these consequences can motivate you to gain greater control over your anger and transform it into healthy skills for living. Experiencing the consequences may help you learn how to rebuild your life and relationships.

Personally, you may be struggling with a lot of regret over your actions as well. Feelings of guilt and shame and remorse may overcome you at times. You may have lost sleep, experienced changes in your appetite or kept ruminating over the events. Learning to deal with these emotions is a consequence as well and can be prevented by transforming your anger into assertiveness, problem-solving, conflict resolution, empathy and forgiveness.

You may still blame your spouse or the other person who you think incited you to anger. You may be dealing with a growing resentment and urge to get revenge. Working through these thoughts and emotions is necessary. You will need to clarify what your responsibility was and is and what the other person's responsibility was and is. You may never be reconciled – if this person was a stranger as in the case of road rage. It's up to you to choose the road of forgiveness versus the road of "getting even."

The most important question you can ask yourself is: "How can I allow the consequences I have incurred to change me so I can experience the benefits of good anger?" What *can* you get out of this?

When you commit to changing your behavior and managing anger you can experience the following:
1. Personal growth and control over my emotions.
2. Improved relational skills and healthier relationships.
3. Greater sense of dignity.

4. Reconciliation with God and others.

5. No fear over further consequences with the law or fear of losing of job, money, relationships, etc.

6. More satisfying life.

7. No shame or guilt because of angry outbursts.

8. Achievement of healthy goals.

9. Growth in Emotional Intelligence.

10. Deeper understanding and intimacy with your partner.

Foundational Insights:

Angry outbursts and hidden anger result in negative consequences and painful relationships. You can motivate yourself to change and take responsibility for your response to angry feelings. You can prevent negative consequences by learning to manage your anger! You can enjoy the benefits of good and healthy anger as you learn assertiveness, empathy, problem-solving and forgiveness!

Questions for Thought

1. What consequences have you incurred because of your anger? What have you lost? How had anger affected your relationship?

_____

_____

2. How has experiencing these consequences motivated you to change especially in your marriage or significant relationship?

_____

_____

3. When have you tried to make amends with your partner for the harm or pain you have caused?

_____

_____

4. If you were to change by consistently managing your anger – how would your life be different? How would your marriage and relationship improve?

_____

_____

5. Describe how have you dealt with the consequences? How has your perspective and behavior changed?

_____

_____

PRACTICE ACTIVITIES

(A) Your partner is frustrated that you came home late or forgot to tell him/her about a conflicting responsibility and says, "you always come late and then dinner is cold!" You say:

Hear:
Paraphrase/mirror your spouse's statement (calmly & respectfully, "what I hear you saying is"):
_____
_____
_____

Empathy: ("you sound frustrated and I can understand that")
_____
_____
_____

Ask: (apologize, clarify, request. "I'm sorry.." "I meant to call you to let you know but, I was delayed.." "I hope you will forgive me..")
_____
_____
_____

Love: ("How can I help you now?")
_____
_____
_____

(B) Your spouse is upset that you are at the computer every evening leaving you little time together as a family.

Hear:
Paraphrase or mirror your spouse's statement (calmly and respectfully, "you feel upset because I am spending little time with the family…"):
_____
_____
_____

Empathy: ("If I were in your shoes – I would feel upset too." "It bothers me that you are so troubled by my behavior.")
_____
_____
_____

Ask: (apologize, clarify, request. "Can you tell me more about how this has affected you?" "What suggestions do you have for changes I can make that will still allow me to finish this extra project?" "I hope you will forgive me..")

_____

_____

_____

Love: ("Is there a way I be more involved and still have time for this project?")

_____

_____

_____

(C) Write out a scenario from your marriage. Your spouse is/says:

_____

_____

Hear:
Paraphrase or mirror your spouse's statement (calmly and respectfully):

_____

_____

_____

Empathy:

_____

_____

_____

Ask: (apologize, clarify, request)

_____

_____

_____

Love:

_____

_____

_____

What if scenarios:
a. *Your partner cracks a joke which causes you to feel disrespected.*
Your anger quotient is: 1-10 (1=low; 5= moderate; 10=high) _____
Your response is:

_____
_____

What's good about your response (thoughts, behavior)?

_____
_____

Describe the consequences of your response:

_____
_____

How does this help you achieve your personal and relationship goals?

_____
_____

What do you need to change? How could applying one of the HEAL skills help the situation?

_____
_____

b. *Your spouse forgets to pay a bill on time and you fear it will affect your credit rating.*
Your anger quotient is: 1-10 (1=low; 5= moderate; 10=high) _____
Your response is:

_____
_____

What's good about your response (thoughts, behavior)?

_____
_____

Describe the consequences of your response:

_____
_____

How does this help you achieve your personal and relationship goals?

_____
_____

What do you need to change? How could applying one of the HEAL skills help the situation?

_____
_____

Cognitive strategies Activity Sheet: These strategies or reminders are used to guide behavior during the provocation itself or to counter irrational beliefs that set the stage for overreaction.

Thinking ahead reminders: The purpose of self-talk reminders is to help you make more deliberate and adaptive choices when confronted with a provocation (Feindler and Ecton). From a neural perspective – you are prompting higher brain center activities located in the verbal left-hemisphere region to control or override emotional reactions of the lower limbic regions.

Reminders interfere with impulsivity in 2 major ways: coping self-talk is an incompatible behavior that blocks the processing of "hot" thoughts. Second, reminders can be prompts to activate predetermined coping efforts. Sample reminders:

Approaching the situation:
Generate alternative response options and weigh the long-term consequences of each. This process has been shown to produce better responses. Rehearse reminders "out loud" during role-play situations.
· Keep your breathing even.
· What is it that I have to do?
· Take one step at a time.
· Stick to the issue and don't take it personally.

During the confrontation:
· Just exhale slowly.
· Remember not to take it personally.
· He/she might want me to get angry but I'm going to one-up him/her by staying cool.
· What is the issue really? Keep it in perspective.
· Just state your needs clearly. Stick to "I" statement. No blaming--that won't help.
· Acknowledge his/her point. That can help sometimes.
· Getting real mad will cost me. I'll be a chump. Stay calm--be a champ.
· No one is right or wrong. We just have different needs.
· If there's nothing I can do now, just chill-out. It will be over soon. Ride the wave.

The following leads may be useful: What would you tell a friend to calm down in a situation?
· What could you tell yourself to "chill-out" your body?
· What would you ideally want to do? What could you say to yourself to accomplish this?

Thinking ahead reminders:
Self-talk can also curb impulsivity by helping the individual anticipate consequences. Thinking ahead reminders or problem solving may be particularly applicable as an individual considers a course of action when there is an impulse to become aggressive. Examples of typical thinking ahead reminders:
• What's going to happen if….
• Is it really worth it?
• Is making myself look tough now worth it for what it'll cost me?
• Will this make a difference in a week?
• What might be some things I could do or say?

Notes

This comprehensive workbook provides several references or paraphrases from the Holy Bible for greater insights and examples into anger and healthy responses to it.

Lesson Two:
1. Ephesians 4:25

Lesson Three:
1. James 1:19
2. Proverbs 22:24
3. Proverbs 15:1

Lesson Five:
1. Nehemiah 5:6-7
2. James 1:19

Lesson Seven:
1. Colossians 3:12-14
2. I Corinthians 13:4-5

Lesson Eight:
1. Colossians 3:13

Lesson Nine:
1. James 1:19

Lesson Ten:
1. Philippians 4:8

BIBLIOGRAPHY

Ali, Dr. Amir. The Article Collection of M. Amir Ali, Ph.D. "Forgiveness." Date of access: February 2, 2006. <http://www.ilaam.net/Forgiveness.html> a personal website.

Backus, William. Hidden Rift With God. Minneapolis, MN: Bethany House, 1990.

Burns, D. Feeling Good. New York: Signet, 1980.

Carlson, Dwight L., M.D. Overcoming Hurts & Anger. Eugene, OR: Harvest House, 1981.

Dobson, Dr. James and Dobson, Shirley. Night Light : A Devotional for Couples. Sisters, OR: Multnomah, Inc., 2000.

Feindler, E.L. and Ecton, R.B. Adolescent Anger Control: Cognitive-Behavioral Techniques. New York: Pergamon Press, 1986.

Gintner, Dr. Gary. Behavioral Anger Reduction Kit (BARK). Louisiana State University, 1995. Used by permission. Email: gintner@lsu.edu. Our thanks to Dr. Gintner for the use of his manual's statistics, anger triggers, the process of anger and thinking ahead reminders.

Goleman, Daniel. Working with Emotional Intelligence. New York: Bantam Books, 2000.

Hauck, Dr. Paul A. Overcoming Frustration and Anger. Westminster John Knox Press; Dimensions, 1974.

Holmes, T.H. and Rahe, R.H. "The Social Readjustment Rating Scale." Journal of Psychosomatic Research, 11:213-218, 1967.

Kendall, R.T. Total Forgiveness. Lake Mary, FL: Charisma House, 2007.

McKay, M., Rogers, P.D. and McKay, J. When Anger Hurts: Quieting the Storm Within. Oakland: New Harbinger, 1989.

Potter-Efron, Ron. Handbook of Anger Management. New York: Haworth Press, 2005.

Potegal, M., Stemmler, G., Spielberger, C. International Handbook of Anger. New York: Springer, 2010.

Prager, Dennis. "Response." The Sunflower. New York: Schocken Books, 1998. 225-30.

Yancey, Philip. "An Unnatural Act." Christianity Today. 8 April 1991: 36-39.

ABOUT THE AUTHORS

Lynette J. Hoy is a Licensed Clinical Professional Counselor in the State of Illinois, a National Certified Counselor and a credentialed Anger Management Specialist-1V, Diplomate, Supervisor and Consultant with the National Anger Management Association. Mrs. Hoy is also a Board Certified Professional Christian Counselor, a crisis counselor and domestic violence advocate.

Lynette has counseled and trained hundreds of clients, couples, and students in anger management. She has trained and certified hundreds of counselors, professionals, and leaders in anger management. Lynette presents various classes, workshops, and marriage seminars. She and her husband, David, have been married over forty years and have one married daughter. Lynette's experience of growing up in an abusive home and then counseling clients struggling with anger has provided the motivation for writing the What's Good About Anger? books, various anger management articles, workbooks, and training manuals. Lynette's faith in Christ and understanding of salvation gave her a foundation for loving and forgiving her father.

Ted Griffin worked as Senior Editor of Crossway Books, a division of Good News Publishers, for thirty years and is currently retired. He has authored numerous gospel tracts, including the best-selling You're Special, and is working on several books. He is a mentor, small group facilitator, and adult Sunday school teacher at Calvary Memorial Church in Oak Park, Illinois. He and his wife, Lois (recently deceased), were married for over 40 years and have two grown children and five grandchildren. Having grown up under an alcoholic father, he has personally struggled with and has extensively studied anger issues.

CONTRIBUTOR

Steve Yeschek is a Licensed Clinical Social Worker in the State of Illinois, and is credentialed as a Certified Anger Management Specialist-1V, Diplomate, Supervisor and Consultant with the National Anger Management Association. Steve is co-presenter of the Anger Management Institute training workshops and co-founder with Lynette of CounselCare Connection, P.C. and the Anger Management Institute in Oak Brook, IL. Steve is the Pastor of Caring Ministries at the Evangelical Free Church of Crystal Lake, IL He has been married to Nancy for 37 years. They live in Cary, Illinois and have 6 children and 3 grandchildren.

Anyone desiring to contact the authors by email is invited to do so:
Lynette Hoy: counselor@hoyweb.com & Ted Griffin: twordsmith@aol.com

Anger Management Institute Resources and Programs

1. What's Good About Anger? First edition: for readers and leaders seeking a Christian perspective on and approach to anger. (2002). Biblical Keys for Transforming Anger Book and Workbook (2013).

2. What's Good About Anger? Putting Your Anger to Work for Good Third Edition (for a general readership) with FAQs. Foreword by Dr. Richard Pfeiffer. (2012)

3. Anger management certificate courses for individuals needing personal growth or who are required to fulfill court or employer orders for anger management.

4. Anger Management Trainer-Specialist Certificate Programs; live workshops; online & home-study courses for counselors, law enforcement or probation officers, educators, professionals, lay leaders and group facilitators. Approved and endorsed by the National Anger Management Association for obtaining certification as an Anger Management Specialist. Workshops approved by NBCC, NASW for 12 CEs/CEUs and IAODAPCA for 13 CEUs. Online and home-study programs approved by NBCC for 15 CEs and IAODAPCA for 12 CEUs.

5. What's Good About Anger? DVDs with Lynette Hoy, NCC, LCPC, CAMS-IV and Steve Yeschek, LCSW, CAMS-IV.

6. What's Good About Anger? Expanded book/workbooks for adults, children & teens. Keys to Defusing Anger and Hostility in Marriage – Book and Workbook for Couples (2013). Healing the Wounds of Anger in Marriage (2015).

Visit the Anger Management Institute site for all resources and the shopping mall at www.whatsgoodaboutanger.com and www.copingwithanger.com for ordering information. For any questions contact Lynette Hoy at 630.368.1880, ext. 1 or lynettehoy@gmail.com

Requests for information should be addressed to:

CounselCare Connection, P.C.
1200 Harger Rd. Suite 602
Oak Brook, Illinois, 60523

Made in the USA
Columbia, SC
02 June 2017